AF584939

BUSH FOODS TO GATHER, COOK AND SHARE WITH THE WHOLE FAMILY

SAMANTHA MARTIN

Hardie Grant
EXPLORE

CONTENTS

INTRODUCTION

ACKNOWLEDGEMENT

I would like to start by acknowledging and expressing my utmost respect for all the traditional lands on which this book gets read. I pay my respects by acknowledging Country in this way to show that I understand and respect I am on someone else's tribal lands, and that I acknowledge the traditional people from past, present and future generations to come.

When I talk about Country, I'm talking about the land, rivers and valleys, and the connections an Indigenous person has to the ancestors of the Country they were born in. As an Aboriginal woman, it is very important for me to acknowledge the lands, waters, seas and tribes or clans in which we live or venture – that way, their ancestral spirits can sense we have only good intentions on their Country, and will protect and guide us while we explore it.

I would also like to pay my respects to you, the person reading my book. May you find comfort in knowing you are taking part in preserving and passing on important knowledge from our rich culture.

Many Aboriginal languages have been lost in the last 150 years and unfortunately the majority of our First Languages are no longer spoken. We are proud Aboriginal and Torres Strait Islander people who are now fighting to regain the knowledge of language and preserve what we can before it is all forgotten. So this is why, as you will notice in this guide, some bush tukka has language names, and some does not.

ABOUT ME

Hi, everyone! My name is Samantha Martin, and I'm also known as the Bush Tukka Woman. My Aboriginal name is Nyudbi, which is a tall white gum tree. I grew up in the East Kimberley region of Western Australia, and I come from the Jaru people, from my mother's tribe.

My mother, Nancy Martin, taught me a lot about bush tukka, and what to eat and what not to eat. We didn't have books like this to help us. I had my mother – she was my book. She taught me about the seasonal changes, and how to identify certain foods in the bush by looking at the shape of the leaves or the texture of the bark. She showed me animal tracks in the sand, and gave me tips for tracking animals like the goanna. Her favourite bush tukka was the bush turkey – but she loved everything caught in the bush! I get my love and passion for bush tukka from my mum!

Growing up in the Kimberley was tough, but those were the best days of my life – no electricity, no running water, just simple living. We lived a long way out of town, in remote communities, mostly on Country with my family. We didn't have the luxury of shops. What I remember is swimming in the most beautiful freshwater holes, and the fun of fishing and hunting for our food.

The best time to go out bush was after the wet season – this was when the rivers, billabongs and creeks were full of fresh rainwater and pumping with fish, turtles and cherubin (freshwater prawns), and the lands were thriving with plums and berries.

We had our favourite spots to go to, like trees we knew had lots of Garlay (green plums). It was great when someone would shake the trees while we stood underneath and the ripe plums rained down on us. The excitement was like opening presents on Christmas Day! We would collect as much as we could as fast as we could, trying to beat the others. The plums were like our lollies – we thought they were the best thing ever.

Beyond living and learning survival skills, I also knew I wanted to have a good education. But that meant I had to leave my community and Country. I spent three years boarding at an all-girls high school in Perth, a very different place and climate from back home. I went from sweltering 40°C heat to sometimes 5°C, which felt freezing! But, even though I missed my family and my Country, I knew that I needed to finish high school and get a good education.

Over the years, I have become a cultural knowledge educator, and offer my services as the Bush Tukka Woman around Australia and the world. This allows me to provide fun programs about cultural bush tukka, including cooking demonstrations and classes. Because I didn't know how to read until Year 12, I especially enjoy working with schools to tackle numeracy and literacy.

I'm passionate about preserving and sharing cultural knowledge and teaching survival skills that could possibly save your life in the outback. I hope to continue inspiring people to explore our rich and diverse bush tukka and what it has to offer – and to have fun doing it!

DEAR BUSH TUKKA EXPLORERS

Learning the basic skills of how to hunt, gather and forage will enrich your knowledge of survival. The most important thing to remember is: **never eat anything that you are not familiar with, and make sure you always seek a second opinion from an Elder who knows about bush foods in your area**.

Not all bush berries and plums are edible, and a lot of things in the bush can harm you if you're not aware of what they are.

But some bush foods are great for us! A lot of them are full of great minerals, vitamins and other nutrients that help our bodies grow and stay healthy. In fact, a lot of our native bush foods have more vitamins than most of the fruits you get in the supermarket! In this guide, I have also created special recipes using bush tukka for you to try.

My people, the Indigenous people of Australia, lived and survived for tens of thousands of years using great hunting, gathering and foraging skills. They learnt what is in season in their areas, when it's a good time to go hunting, and how to read the signs of the landscape and the moon cycle to work out when it's the best time to hunt certain animals. Having these skills can help you too, to navigate in different parts of the country.

By reading *Bush Tukka Guide for Kids*, you are playing a big part in preserving this cultural knowledge. You are seeking ancient wisdom to help you with your bush tukka discovery, and I am extremely happy I can assist you on your journey.

Love from

The Bush Tukka Woman

SO, WHAT IS BUSH TUKKA?

Being Aboriginal plays an important role in my life story, with the love I have for bush tukka. I feel it is my obligation to share and preserve that knowledge. My fondest childhood memories are learning from my Elders about how they survived the harsh climates, from droughts to flooding, from freezing cold to unbearable heat. They did not have the luxury of cars, houses or electricity to run air-conditioning or fridges. They battled the elements.

My people are the oldest living culture on this planet, and that says a lot about their survival skills and resilience! We understand that the land, rivers and sea are our greatest source of nature's wild foods – a source that we have access to whenever we want.

Before you read on, I would like you to find a place where you can sit and close your eyes. Now, imagine you are in your town, but there are no houses, no cars, no schools, no shops, not a building in sight. There are just lots of trees, bushlands and animals. Then, I want you to imagine that you are very hungry and that you really need to eat – but remember, there are no shops! How would you feel? What do you think you would do? Would you be brave enough to hunt an animal like a goanna or kangaroo? Would you have the skills to find water or plums or berries? If you're not sure what you'd do, then this guide will help! It is a good place to start learning basic skills and knowledge.

In this guide, you will also learn that there are a lot of plants and animals that are poisonous. It's very important to make sure you get the right information before you put anything in your mouth. My ancestors used vigorous processes before they ate certain plants or animals, to make sure all the toxins had been released first.

A simple but very important tip my mother taught me was never eat something without putting it to the tip of your tongue first, because it's easier to treat an itchy or stingy tongue then an extremely upset stomach. This simple technique helped my people gain knowledge and know what to eat, and what not to eat.

In my heart, there is an urgency for Aboriginal People to preserve our cultural knowledge so it is not lost. We must find as many different ways as possible to teach, pass on and record our knowledge. I hope this book sparks an interest in you to discover, learn and hopefully help preserve our people's way of life.

Bush tukka is not just plants. We must also acknowledge the Ngarla (meats) of our primary bush foods. My people gain nutrients from the proteins of the food. We eat everything, and nothing goes to waste. Bush foods and bush medicine are both so valuable. In the days of traditional bush living, my ancestors were lean, healthy and muscular. You can see how their diets and hunting-and-gathering practices provided them with pure energy and nutrients, unlike the processed foods we all eat today.

Now, just think about how different hunting in the bush is from 'hunting' for food in supermarket aisles, where all the meats have been already killed, skinned, gutted and cut up nice and neat. How can traditional hunting, which takes time and energy, compete with the ease of buying what you want from a supermarket? Eating too much processed food is making my mob sick with things like diabetes, liver problems and heart disease. A lot of this is because people don't know as much as they could about bush foods.

I want to inspire you to not be afraid of introducing bush tukka into your life and your kitchen. I have included plants and animals from all over Australia, and I hope you will use this book as a tool to identify different bush foods when you are out and about. After all, we have some of the healthiest and most nutritious foods in our bush backyard, and our oldest living culture has lived and survived for thousands of years on these foods. If they can, why can't we?

Happy hunting and gathering, Bush Tukka Explorers!

TEACHINGS FROM MY ANCESTORS

SHARED KNOWLEDGE

Australia is a big country with a big history, and diverse cultures, geography and climate. We need to start by understanding that there are over 250 Indigenous language groups with 800 different dialects. And, within each language group, there are different stories, customs and ceremonies. These stories connect us to everything from the plants and animals to the land formations to the rivers and valleys.

Each language group has a Dreaming story, and while these stories are all different they are also in some senses very similar. One story that is shared by many is how the world was created by the rainbow serpent, which shaped the landscape and created the rivers and valleys. For example, if you're in a plane and look out the window, you will notice the rivers are not straight, they are windy – just like a snake travelling along the land.

You might be asking, 'How can a snake or serpent create such rivers and mountains?' Well, back in the Dreaming, the serpent was a giant – it was bigger than mountains! – which is how it could travel so far across the lands, and why it left an indent in the landscape that we now call the riverbeds. Even in the dry season, you can see the shape of the serpent's body. While it moved across the lands, it shifted the landscape, creating hills along the way. It also shed its colourful scales, which created the gemstones (opals) found around the country.

COUNTRY

Our bushlands are home to a lot of plants and wildlife that are edible (meaning you can eat them), and a lot that are poisonous (meaning you can't eat them).

However, identifying the edible plants in different areas of Australia is not exactly easy. It is good to understand how unique the landscapes are right across the country – this knowledge will help you to identify plants and where they best grow.

It's funny when I hear people say all plants look the same. They don't really! People who have survival knowledge can identify edible plants and medicines just by looking at the texture of the bark, or the shape and colour of the leaves, or even the flowers.

It's also good to know the changes in the landscape where these plants grow and what climate they thrive in. Aboriginal and Torres Strait Islander People have a deep spiritual connection to land and the environment, and identify with where they were born. For instance, I'm a freshwater person. (See page XXII for more information.)

HISTORY

Aboriginal People have lived and survived off these great southern lands for over 65,000 years, and have learnt how to acknowledge and respect the Country and the animals and the seasonal changes.

Prior to colonisation (when people started coming to Australia from Europe), Aboriginal People lived here proudly and held significant knowledge of tracking, hunting and gathering skills. They lived in clan groups of as many as 40 to 60 people. Clans respected each other's boundaries, and would seek permission to come into another clan's territory to trade tools and hunting weapons, and sometimes food.

Generally, the men born into the clan were responsible for protecting and feeding the community. Hunting would take them away from their family for days, sometimes weeks, depending on the food source. They would track and hunt larger game animals like emu, bush turkey, kangaroo, deer, goanna or sometimes crocodile.

While the men were away, the women would feed the clan, and hunt smaller game, like rock wallaby, goanna, fish, turtle and echidna, and forage for bush fruits and roots. The women also kept the community safe. They looked after the children and the Elders, and were responsible for keeping peace and balance in the families.

The children also played an important role in the community. They would look after their Elders, collect wood, help make the fire and keep it going. They also looked out for the younger kids while they played happily in the waterholes or around the camp. Boys aged between 10 and 13 had more of a responsibility to ensure the community was looked after while the men went away – this was their rite of passage into manhood.

The men would only return when they could bring back enough food for the whole tribe, and they only took what they needed from the land – nothing more. Every part that could be eaten was eaten. Nothing went to waste. They used everything the animal provided, including the fur, bones, sinew, teeth, feathers and claws for costumes and weaponry.

They also honoured the lives of the animals they ate, and took on the strength or speed of that animal. But if the animal was someone's totem, that person was not allowed to eat, kill or harm it.

A totem is a very special thing. A member of the clan receives their totem either at birth, or from the Elders. If you are given a totem at birth, this would mean your mother or father ate that animal and you would take on its spirit.

WATER

Australia is one of the driest lands in the world, but Aboriginal People knew exactly where and how to find water. They knew how to watch animals, such as a flock of birds, which would lead them to water in the early morning and late afternoon.

They also knew how to find underwater bores and springs, which they used as reliable water sources. They would cover the holes with huge rocks, or sticks and leaves, to keep animals from drinking or contaminating the water.

My ancestors knew it was important to camp close to water for drinking, eating and bathing. The clans set up camp by waterholes, which also provided an endless supply of foods such as freshwater prawns, turtles, fish, eels, waterlilies and mussels. Waterholes also offered a cooling-off spot for the children and women. In the wet season, clans would venture up to higher ground so they wouldn't get caught in the floods.

PLANTS

We are very lucky to live in such a beautiful, diverse country. Not only diverse in people, landscapes and environments but also in flora (plant species). Australian flora includes lots of ecologically significant species, such as acacia, eucalyptus, melaleuca and grevillea. The acacias tend to grow more in drier inland parts of Australia, while the eucalyptus and melaleucas grow more in wetter parts.

The vegetation in our country plays an important role in the ecosystem. It is a great resource, and helps Aboriginal People know where to look for bush tukka. For example, in the northern parts of Australia, mangroves, savannahs, and tropical and subtropical rainforests offer an abundance of bush tukka and bush medicines, such as mud crabs, mussels, oysters and snails. And the freshwater wetlands offer freshwater turtles, ducks, magpie geese and more.

ANIMALS

Australia's best-known animals are the kangaroo, echidna and emu. But did you know that there are more than 378 species of mammal, 828 species of bird, 300 species of lizard and 140 species of snake? Meanwhile, there are only two species of crocodile – freshwater and saltwater.

Of the mammals, almost half are marsupials (pouched mammals, like the kangaroo). The rest are either monotremes (egg-laying mammals, like the echidna) or placental mammals (all other mammals).

OUR LAND, OUR COUNTRY

OUR LANDSCAPE

Understanding the different environments in Australia is one of the most important survival skills you need. The landscape changes dramatically and plays an important part within Indigenous cultures. Looking and learning about changes in our landscape helps us understand what food and resources are available.

The southern half of Australia has a different landscape from the northern tropics. The south has a more Mediterranean climate; an arid coastline; cold, wet winters and hot, dry summers. In comparison, most of Australia's northern tropical regions contain areas of mangrove swamps, rainforest, woodland, grassland and desert.

DESERT PEOPLE

The desert people of Australia are among the greatest hunters and gatherers. Having the skills, knowledge and understanding of where to find food and water in the desert is extraordinary. You might think nothing grows in the desert because it's hot and appears to have no life or food. But to the desert people, finding bush tukka is as easy as shopping in a supermarket! They know how to find underground springs for water, where to dig for wild yams, and how to find honey ants, witchetty grubs, echidnas and sand goannas.

Growing up in the desert is harsh, and dealing with the heat is difficult and exhausting. The temperature changes from extreme heat during the day to freezing at night. Now, the modern world makes it easier to get around the desert, allowing desert people to travel across their Country more quickly.

Desert people have great Dreaming stories of their Country. They depict hunting and gathering stories through their traditional dance and vibrant artwork. This shows how important it is for Elders to teach younger generations about what they eat off their lands and how they survive.

RAINFOREST PEOPLE

Rainforest people are custodians of the forests. They have lived among some of the oldest trees on our planet. Learning to survive in damp, cool, wet terrains, they have adapted to their dense, lush green surroundings. With fresh waterways readily accessible, they have learned different methods of how to trap fish, prawns, eels and turtles.

The men and women catch prawns by scooping out handfuls of leaves from the small waterholes where they live, then grabbing the prawns before they scurry back into the water. They also use a plant known as foam bark tree (*Jagera pseudorhus*) to stun fish, by crushing the leaves, putting them in dilly bags and soaking the leaves in still waterholes. This takes the oxygen out of the water and the fish float to the surface, where the rainforest people gather them. (The poison does not harm humans.)

The rainforest people also delight in hunting scrub hens and collecting their eggs from nesting mounds – they make nets out of strong fibres from the inner bark of the fig tree to capture the hens. They also gather and eat wild berries, plums, roots, seeds, nuts and yams when in season, and only take what they need.

During the wet season the rainforest people move towards drier environments to escape the wet, damp and cold landscape, where it becomes difficult to hunt food. Then they return to the rainforest in the dry season, when they need to cool down from the scorching heat.

FRESHWATER PEOPLE

I come from the freshwater and saltwater people, located inland. My landscape is rugged mountains cut with ancient sandstones and limestones gorges, freshwater waterfalls and rivers. The Cambridge Gulf pours massive high tides of saltwater into the Kimberley Five Rivers, filling the creeks and valleys with saltwater.

Freshwater people live inland from the coast, surrounded by vast lands. They rely on freshwater wetlands, swamps, rivers, creeks, waterholes and billabongs to catch many species of fish, turtle, eel and prawn.

The freshwater people have a deep spiritual and cultural connection to these waterholes. The rainforest people believe that a powerful spirit sleeps at the bottom of the waterholes and should be respected and not disturbed.

Waterholes like rivers, creeks and billabongs offer a protected and peaceful environment for the tribes. They can fish on a daily basis and gather under the cool, shaded paperbark and eucalyptus trees. The women and children also spend time swimming and collecting mussels from the banks and prawns from the rivers. But they also understand that setting up their camps by waterholes brings the danger of crocodiles, so always keep out a watchful eye out!

SALTWATER PEOPLE

Saltwater people live on the coastal fringes or islands of Australia. Their hunting is ruled by the sea and tides, but they also have an impressive knowledge of the ocean environment. They have a deep spiritual and cultural connection to the sea and the ocean, and believe that if they disrespect the ocean it will not provide them with fish.

Saltwater people hunt in mangroves swamps, estuaries, rivers and beaches, and along reefs. Coastal saltwater people delight in collecting different varieties of shellfish, including oysters off the rocks, mud mussels and mangrove snails from the mangroves, and cockles from beneath the sand and rock pools. They thrive on the diverse and abundant marine life.

Coastal people have hunting tools for spearing fish, stingrays, crabs and turtles. Most shellfish and fresh fish are caught and cooked before being eaten, but there are a few animals that are eaten fresh, such as mangrove worms and oysters. Turtle eggs can be drunk to quench thirst too.

THE TROPICAL ZONES

In northern Australia, there are three different tropical climates with unique weather patterns. The two main seasons are the wet and dry seasons.

ZONE ONE: EQUATORIAL

This zone ranges from the tip of Cape York Peninsula to Bathurst, Melville Island, and the north of Darwin in the Northern Territory.

ZONE TWO: TROPICAL

This zone spreads right across the northern regions of Australia, including Cape York (again), the top end of the Northern Territory, areas south of the Gulf of Carpentaria, and the Kimberley region of Western Australia.

ZONE THREE: SUBTROPICAL

This zone covers the coastal and inland fringe from Cairns along the Queensland coast and hinterland to the northern areas of New South Wales, and the coastal fringe north of Perth to Geraldton in Western Australia.

THE WET AND DRY SEASONS

Around the world, everyone is familiar with the four seasons that change every three months: summer, autumn, winter and spring. In the tropical zones of northern Australia, there are only two key seasons: the wet season and the dry season. These seasons last for approximately six months each.

The wet season is also known as the monsoon season. Rain clouds start to build up around August but the downpour is in November through to March. It is actually hotter than the dry season, with temperatures soaring from 30–50°C. This is caused by the high humidity and build-up of moisture in the air from all the flooding.

The dry season is exactly that – everything is so dry! It starts around April and lasts through to October. With clear blue skies, the temperature reaches around 20°C, but it is so dry that the sun's rays dry up the land, grass and waterholes.

The build-up to the wet season lasts three or four months. This is the humid time of the year – the time when everyone becomes edgy as they swelter in the humidity and wait for the first rains. People in the Cape York region call the first rain the mango rain, because it gives the mango trees a drink as they start to bear fruit. People in the Kimberley region call it the silly season as people tend to do silly things because of the heat, which lasts all day and all night with no break! When the rains finally fall they bring welcome relief, cooling everything down.

During extreme flooding in the wet season, it's difficult to get around as the ground becomes boggy. This generally means hunting season is over for a few months. Before this time of the year, Aboriginal People prepare themselves and stock up on food and water.

Back in the days of our ancestors, at this time of the year everyone headed for the hilltops to live in warm and dry caves. From up there, they also had a full view of the vast lands below and would sometimes travel back down when they needed to hunt for large animals to feed the tribe.

Aboriginal People in the tropical zone in the Northern Territory and Kimberley areas rely on a basic seasonal calendar. This helps them to map out the hunting and gathering seasons, based on what is in and out of season. It also helps them to prepare for extreme weather events, such as cyclones, flooding, storms and bushfires, which affect the road access and the livelihood of the community.

WET SEASON

DRY SEASON

A BUSH TUKKA GARDEN

Children, educators and parents often ask me which bush tukka plants are the best to grow in pots or gardens. So, here is a list of my five favourites, plus ideas and information to get you started on your very own bush tukka garden! It can become a sacred space and community hub, a place where you share culture at the same time as providing food and medicine. How deadly is that!

CREATING YOUR SPACE

First, choose where you are going to grow your bush tukka garden. If you are creating it at home but don't have an open yard, it might be in pots or a planter box. Or, if it's a community or school project, you might have a larger area to use. If you have space to invite your community's Elders to participate, I would recommend including a yarning or fire pit so they can come, sit and tell stories.

Growing native edible plants involves a bit of effort. You will need to make sure that your environment is appropriate, and the soil is healthy, well drained and loaded with enough organic matter.

If your garden is bigger, you will also need to think about how it will be watered and how the water will drain from it – this is something that adults can help with. If you are growing a small garden in pots, use good potting mix and water your plants with a hose or watering can.

Also remember that most plants thrive on sunlight! Most need good morning or afternoon sun to grow. So, when you are planning your space, remember to ensure your plants will get some sunlight – not *too* much, but enough to provide them with the light energy they need for photosynthesis.

When you have chosen your plants, you might like to make signs to display their Aboriginal name/s. You could also paint the pots or boxes your plants will grow in, create decorative stepping stones for your garden, or a sign that says 'Welcome to my garden'.

DID YOU KNOW?

Photosynthesis is the process by which plants use sunlight, water and carbon dioxide to create oxygen and energy in the form of sugar.

CHOOSING YOUR PLANTS

The best way to make sure your garden is a success is to grow plants that are suitable for your climate. Contact your local Elders or nurseries for information on what types of native bush plants grow in your area. This website is a great resource: tuckerbush.com.au

Once most plants are big enough, they will happily grow without much attention. However, feeding them frequently with some sort of plant food (seaweed or liquid fertiliser, for example) will encourage good growth and intense flavour. Lots of nurseries can give you advice about caring for and feeding native edible plants.

Here are five of my favourite native plants to grow. Please keep in mind that not all will be available at every store or nursery all year round, due to seasonal availability.

LEMON MYRTLE

I refer to lemon myrtle as the Queen of the Herbs. It can be grown in a large pot, but thrives in the ground. It grows well in subtropical rainforest regions that are warm with cool winds, and semi-dry areas. Choose a location with soil that drains well and receives full sun. Keep it free of frost and well watered throughout the year and it will flourish. (See page 30 for main entry.)

FINGER LIME

Finger limes are native to south-east Queensland and northern New South Wales and grow 6–10m high, as a big shrub or small tree. They grow well in subtropical cool and moist environments, and in full sun to moderate shade in warm areas. You can even grow a finger lime in a pot!

MIDYIM BERRY

Midyim plants are hardy and self-sufficient and don't take up a lot of room, making them easy to care for. They grow naturally in sandy coastal areas, woodland, and subtropical and rainforest fringes. In their natural habitat they can reach a height of 2m, however often grow to only 50cm high and 80cm wide. Choose a spot in your garden where your midyim plant will get full sun or light shade and have well-drained soil. (See page 34 for main entry.)

OLD MAN SALTBUSH

This distinctive silver-grey shrub grows quickly, reaching 1–3m high and 2–5m wide. It grows naturally in coastal areas, woodland, and subtropical and rainforest fringes. In your garden, saltbush can grow in full sun or partial shade, but needs to be protected from strong frosts. The flowers are male and female, and grow on different plants. Female flowers form thick clusters about 20cm long, while male blooms are round and swarm the ends of each branch. You can grow saltbush in the ground, or in smaller pots if harvested frequently. (See page 38 for main entry.)

LILLY PILLY

Also known as riberry, this species grows naturally in riverine, coastal, subtropical and tropical rainforest environments. Most lilly pillies are grown as decorative trees or hedges because they are hardy and require little care to thrive. As hedges they can grow up to 10m high, but in the wild they can grow up to 15m high! Choose a spot in your garden with full sun or partial shade and well-drained soil. You can also grow lilly pilly in a pot, just make sure it's a nice big one!

PLANTS

BLUE QUANDONG

ABORIGINAL NAME/S

Murrgan – Djabugay tribe, Kuranda, Far North Queensland

BOTANICAL NAME

Elaeocarpus angustifolius

Blue quandong trees are native to the rainforest areas of south-east Queensland and northern New South Wales. They grow well in the moist soil of subtropical rainforests, mostly around water systems such as rivers or creek lines. These giants are easy to spot among other trees because they soar as high as 50m into the sky, and also because their glossy dark-green leaves grow up to 18cm long. These leaves turn from green to a vibrant red just before they fall to the ground.

They start flowering in autumn in the south and early summer in the north, and their clusters of bell-shaped green-white petals are a delicious treat for rainbow lorikeets.

The fruits are bright blue and can grow to 2cm in diameter – a bit bigger than a blueberry. They have a thin layer of green flesh under the skin that tastes bitter and floury, and are best eaten while fresh. Once they dry out, these fruits don't taste as nice! They are a popular treat for the native wildlife, especially flying foxes, woompoo pigeons and cassowaries.

DID YOU KNOW?

Stories have been told by rainforest people in Far North Queensland that the cassowary got its blue colouring from eating too many blue quandongs!

TRADITIONAL USES

The blue quandong stone is hard, brown and has grooves all around it, like a walnut. It is used by local Aboriginal women to make necklaces.

The fruits, although very dry in texture, keep you hydrated for hours. Traditionally, Aboriginal women and children would scrape off the flesh by the river and make a paste out of it, which they ate when they needed to hydrate.

OTHER USES

People have been known to use blue quandongs to make pickles and jams. With a bitter, tangy flavour, these are great to use in stews with red meats.

BOAB NUT

ABORIGINAL NAME/S

Joongari – Wilinggin tribe, East Kimberley region, Western Australia

BOTANICAL NAME

Adansonia gregorii

Boab trees are a Kimberley icon, growing from the west coast right across to the east into the Northern Territory. Every boab tree is unique – they can be tall and skinny, or fat and round, and anywhere from 10–15m tall and 9–12m wide. They are also known as the bottle tree because of their shape.

The star-shaped leaves are a bright lime and dark green. These leaves drop off in the dry season, then grow again around September or early October, and the plant is ready to flower in November.

The flowers start as light-cream pods, then the petals peel back to reveal long brush-like blooms that smell magnificent. The flowers open early in the evening and are pollinated that night, and last only one or two days before falling to the ground.

Boab nuts are hard pods with light-brown fur that can make your skin itchy. Inside is a powdery white pith, containing at least 10–20 seeds. You can eat this – it has a sherbet-like texture and a sour, tangy flavour.

TRADITIONAL USES

Aboriginal People make strong, thick twine from the bark. They also get water from them by banging the trunk until it softens, then stripping off the stringy fibres and wringing them out to release the water. They use the fruits as food and medicine, and the pod shells to collect water and use as bowls and utensils.

Traditionally, young or unripe fruits were buried in warm ground to make them ripe. To create a sweet treat, Aboriginal People crush the pith and seeds, and mix them with water and bush sugarbag (see page 16) droplets. This is very tasty!

Unripe nuts, which are still soft and sticky, can be roasted on hot coals. They taste similar to roasted wild yams – sweet, warm and mushy. The seeds can also be dried and eaten like peanuts.

OTHER USES

The fruits can be used to make chocolates, muffins, bread and cakes. Dried boab flakes can be sprinkled over salads to add tang. The nuts can be used to make jams and chutneys.

BOTTLEBRUSH

ABORIGINAL NAME/S

Birdak – Noongar tribe, Western Australia

BOTANICAL NAME

Callistemon

These shrubs have many names but are most commonly known as bottlebrushes. There are over 40 different species across the eastern and southern parts of Australia, and they come in all sorts of colours. However, the crimson bottlebrush is the most popular.

The natural habitats for bottlebrushes are in Australia's tropical north to the moderate southern lands. They can also be found growing in swamps or wet environments, such as along creek beds or areas that flood.

The spectacular flowers appear in late winter and spring, and resemble a brush for cleaning bottles. Their nectar is absolutely irresistible to birds and insects!

The seeds of the bottlebrush are tiny, hard and bubble-like. They sit on the flower stem in a little cluster.

The leaves of many bottlebrushes are ornamental. In some species, they are even covered with fine, soft hairs. They release a lemony scent when bruised, but be careful handling them. You'll also find them to be very hardy and spiky, so they can prick you if pressed too hard!

DID YOU KNOW?

Bottlebrushes can be red, cream, yellow or pink, and each bloom is in fact made up of a number of individual flowers called filaments.

TRADITIONAL USES

The sweet nectar has always been eaten by Aboriginal People. You can bang the flowers on your hand to release the nectar, then lick it off.

OTHER USES

You can boil the flowers in hot water to create a sweet lemon-scented tea – as the water turns brown, it's ready to drink. This makes for a refreshing and natural drink.

BUNYA NUT

ABORIGINAL NAME/S

Bunyi bunyi – Kabi Kabi tribe, Sunshine Coast, Queensland

BOTANICAL NAME

Araucaria bidwillii

Over time, the Kabi Kabi word 'bunyi bunyi' turned into 'bunya'. These trees grow from Far North Queensland to northern New South Wales. They can reach as high as 45m and are found in subtropical rainforests and the moist soil of land away from the coast, mostly on mountain tops.

The rough bark on their trunks protects them from the cold winds. Their sharp-pointed dark-green leaves are about 2.5cm long, and they produce large green cones about the same size as a football that weigh approximately 10kg! These cones can be found from late January to early March.

A female cone produces 50–100 bunya nuts, which grow inside beige shells held together around the stem by a waxy white sap. Each shell contains one teardrop-shaped bunya nut approximately 6cm long.

To remove the shells, simply pull them off from the base. The easiest way to get to the actual bunya nuts is to boil the shells for up to 30 minutes, either until the water turns slightly brown or when each shell develops a small split at the tip. You can then open the shells with a knife.

TRADITIONAL USES

Bunya nuts were a staple food of Aboriginal People living in south-east Queensland, and were eaten raw or roasted on hot coals. Every year in bunya season, nuts were collected for a bunya gathering and feasting among the tribes. Young Aboriginal warriors would climb the rough-barked trees to get the young cones.

This ceremony was taken extremely seriously and only the fittest warriors were chosen. Climbing a bunya tree is extremely challenging, because the sharp bark can slice your foot if you don't know the correct techniques.

OTHER USES

Bunya nuts are very versatile. Eaten raw, they are crunchy and taste slightly sweet – similar to eating a raw sweet potato. Cooked, they look like giant pine nuts and taste similar to chestnuts – sweet with a floury, waxy texture.

BURDEKIN PLUM

ABORIGINAL NAME/S

Guybalam – Djabugay tribe, Kuranda, Far North Queensland

BOTANICAL NAME

Pleiogynium timorense

Burdekin plum trees belong to the mango family and can grow as high as 30m. They are mostly found along coastal areas, creek banks and in rainforest areas in tropical Far North Queensland.

These distinctive trees have dark, rough bark and strong trunks that are grey in patches. The leaves range in colour from dark to light green, and grow to about 10cm long and 4–6cm wide. Eight to 10 leaves grow on a single stalk, and the flowers are small, creamy-white constellations.

The plums grow on the long, rubbery-looking branches in bunches of 2–10, sometimes more. They appear in winter months, and are deep purple, almost black. Usually the size of a 50-cent piece, they can vary in size depending on the environment.

A thin layer of purple flesh surrounds a large, hard, woody seed, and the fruit is tart in flavour – the riper it is, the sweeter the flavour. But instead of ripening on the trees, these plums ripen from the temperature of the ground when they fall.

TRADITIONAL USES

Burdekin plums are still very popular with local Aboriginal People, who enjoy eating the tangy plums fresh or cooked. Traditionally, the women and children would crush the plums into a paste and, because the fruit is made up of approximately 70 per cent water, it offered a great way to hydrate on hot days.

OTHER USES

Burdekin plums are used for making jams, jellies, cakes and cookies. They also make great chutneys, and savoury or sweet sauces that go well with pork, chicken, lamb and beef. They contain vitamin C and are high in fibre and other natural minerals.

BUSH PASSIONFRUIT

ABORIGINAL NAME/S

Yidiringgi – Jaru tribe, Western Desert, East Kimberley, WA

BOTANICAL NAME

Passiflora foetida

This plant is actually an introduced species, but I've included it as it's become a favourite for many Aboriginal People. It is a weed-like vine that grows over other trees and shrubs, and is commonly found in northern parts of Australia, from the borders of Byron Bay in New South Wales across to Port Hedland in Western Australia. Bush passionfruit thrives in warm, humid and dry tropical weather around rocky hills, swamps, creeks, riverbeds and coastal areas – wherever there is a water system.

Like the vine, the leaves are waxy in texture. Each leaf has three points, similar to the common passionfruit leaf, and the flowers look like delicate orchids. Each one is a mixture of white, light and dark purples, and light and dark greens.

The passionfruit itself grows inside a delicate furry casing that looks a bit like a net. This casing starts off lime green, then changes to bright orange or yellow. Inside the casing is a soft, grey, juicy flesh with about 5–7 black seeds. The fruit is best eaten during summer. Do not eat the fruits when they are green, as they are highly toxic at this stage.

TRADITIONAL USES

Aboriginal People eat everything – the skin and seeds – but because the shell is very thin, the seeds can also be sucked out.

OTHER USES

Wild bush passionfruit vines are everywhere, so they are easily accessible to anyone who would like to try the sweet golden fruits. They work well raw on cheese platters or in fruit salads – just wash them and drop them in whole, or squeeze the seeds over the fruit salad.

If you dry the flowers out, they make a great bedtime tea.

BUSH SUGARBAG

ABORIGINAL NAME/S

Ngarlu – Jaru tribe, Western Desert, East Kimberley, Western Australia
Guku – Yolŋu tribe, Arnhem Land, Northern Territory

SCIENTIFIC NAME

Austroplebeia australis (previously called *Trigona australis*)

There are over 1500 species of native bees in Australia, and only 10 are non-stinging bees, also known as social native bees. These bees produce bush sugarbag. Due to the decline of native bees, we do not encourage the harvesting of bush sugarbag anymore.

Social native bees look more like flies. They are about half a centimetre long, blue-black in colour, and have hairy, extended back legs that carry the nectar and pollen. They are found in warmer tropical areas, and are attracted to native plants. They can live in artificial nests with good, warm insulation, but hollow logs make the best nests. These bees are not aggressive, but if you disturb their nests they will swarm around you and stick to your skin or hair.

Bush sugarbag is dark brown in colour, and can be found in tree hollows where social native bees have made their nests. The bees produce and store small amounts of bush sugarbag with dark-brown wax, and it tastes tangy but has a delicious bush-flower aroma. The honey pods are different from commercial bee pods – they look like a bunch of round, golden-brown grapes.

TRADITIONAL USES

Aboriginal People can spot beehives high up in trees. It can be as simple as seeing a small waxy hole at the end of a branch, or noticing the small black bees buzzing in and out of the hole. I have known my Aunties to follow a single bee to its hive – which is a difficult thing to do out in the bush!

Aboriginal People use the honey as a sweetener, but they also eat it to treat sore throats, and smear it over infected wounds or skin rashes.

Traditionally, men would harvest the wax, then chew it and squeeze it to remove the honey. Then they would heat the wax and mould it over wooden handles to attach an axe head. Finally, they would bind them both in place with natural twine. The wax is also still used for the mouthpieces on didgeridoos, or Yidakis.

OTHER USES

Bush sugarbag can be used like common honey – as a spread on bread, or added to your cooking, salads, cereals or in teas.

BUSH TOMATO

ABORIGINAL NAME/S

Eerlud – Wilinggin tribe, East Kimberley, Western Australia

BOTANICAL NAME

Solanum centrale

This small desert plant, which is approximately 30cm high, has grey-bronze leaves and mauve-blue flowers. It grows well in the dry climates throughout the central deserts – from Tennant Creek in the Northern Territory to Marla in South Australia and the East Kimberley in Western Australia.

In the red sandy desert, the bush tomato plant grows quickly after summer rains, mainly from dormant roots. These roots can last for many years between good growing seasons! The plant will also grow rapidly where soil is disturbed along roadsides and after bushfires.

In the wild, bush tomato plants fruit for only two months. And, although there are 100 species of wild tomato in Australia, only six are edible. The others are highly toxic, and contain high levels of solanine, which is poisonous. It can cause severe stomach aches, vomiting, diarrhoea and can even be fatal. Always seek information from a knowledgeable grown-up before harvesting or eating.

Eerlud, or desert tomatoes, are the best known and most consumed species of edible bush tomato. They are yellow when ripe, and taste sweet and slightly tangy. They grow up to 3cm in diameter.

TRADITIONAL USES

The traditional way to harvest bush tomato is to collect the sun-dried fruits off the bush in autumn and winter. In its dried form, bush tomato can be stored for several years.

Aboriginal People also use the roots to treat toothache. The roots can be baked in ash, then peeled, crushed and placed on the aching tooth. These fruits are believed to build immunity, while also nourishing and hydrating the body from the heat. But don't eat too many, or you might get sick!

OTHER USES

The dried fruit is normally ground and used as a seasoning, rather than eaten whole. It has a strong flavour, so you only need to use a little.

CLUSTER FIG

ABORIGINAL NAME/S

Ngalga-yarrubadjal – Djabugay tribe, Kuranda, Far North Queensland

BOTANICAL NAME

Ficus racemosa

The cluster fig tree is a majestic giant, reaching 35m high and with large green leaves. It grows in forests along riverbanks and in much drier environments with underground water systems, and is found mostly in Western Australia, Northern Territory, the Gulf of Carpentaria and north-east and south-east Queensland. Cluster fig trees are an important part of the ecosystem, providing food for humans and animals, natural medicines and shade along waterways.

These magnificent trees are easy to recognise because the figs grow in clusters on the branches and trunks. The figs are produced from around September to December, and the clusters change colour at different times – from light green to yellow, orange and then red when the fruits are ripe.

The figs that grow on the tree's outside roots are very sweet and, like common figs, have hundreds of seeds inside. But the cluster figs are often infested with insects and larvae, so best check before taking a bite!

TRADITIONAL USES

As well as relying on the fruits as a main food source, Aboriginal People also use other parts of the tree for medicine, and to make tools and canoes. They scrape off the inner bark, then boil it in water to produce a liquid that is good for treating diarrhoea. To make canoes and coolamons, they hollow out the soft inner part of the trunk, because the wood is light, strong and waterproof.

OTHER USES

The cluster fig tree provides great shade and attracts an array of wildlife, from birds to insects. Just make sure not to plant one near buildings, paving, sewer lines or houses, as its roots grow extremely fast and will damage whatever is in the way!

Cluster figs work well in jams and chutneys. You can also bake them, then drizzle them with a syrupy sauce and serve with ice-cream for a delicious dessert.

DAVIDSON'S PLUM

ABORIGINAL NAME/S

Ooray – Jirrbal (Dyirbal) tribe, Far North Queensland
Munumba – Djabugay tribe, Kuranda, Far North Queensland
Jirirr – Kuku Yalanji tribe, Far North Queensland

BOTANICAL NAME

Davidsonia pruriens

Ooray, or Davidson's plums, grow on tall, slender trees with no branches. Most trees reach about 10m high, but they can grow as high as 20m in their natural rainforest environment in Queensland and New South Wales. The unique glossy green leaves are large and feather-like, with thick rib veins and spiky edges.

From November to February, clusters of red and yellow flower blossoms appear on stems off the trunk. Dangling from under the canopy of the droopy umbrella leaves, the fruits start to develop from February to May, and continue to grow and ripen through to August or September. These incredible fruits start off a pale-green colour that later turns to a deep black-purple with a waxy coating on the outside. The flesh inside is a vibrant red with no seeds. When ripe, they will naturally fall to the ground.

Davidson's plums look plump and sweet, but don't be fooled! They are actually very sour and tart.

TRADITIONAL USES

For thousands of years, Aboriginal People have eaten these plums fresh from the tree for hydration. They contain vitamins that can help sores, inflammation and viral infections, and they can also be used to cool burns and stings.

OTHER USES

Ooray are most commonly used in jams, relishes, chutneys, syrups and even wines. Since the fruit is so sour, it needs a lot of sugar to balance the bitterness! They are a superfruit, full of antioxidants, vitamin C, potassium, lutein, vitamin E, folate, zinc, magnesium and calcium.

GREEN PLUM

ABORIGINAL NAME/S

Garlay – Wilinggin tribe,
East Kimberley, Western Australia

BOTANICAL NAME

Buchanania obovata

Garlay (green plum) trees grow as tall as 10m, and have round-edged light-green leaves that are about 12cm long. They are found in rugged terrains close to creeks and rivers, and commonly grow in the eastern part of the Kimberley in Western Australia, and in the Top End of the Northern Territory.

Delicate creamy-white flowers start to appear on Garlay trees in September, in the middle of the wet season. Then they fruit from

October to April – from the end of the wet season until the end of the dry season.

The Garlay plum is round, light green and about the size of a five-cent piece. It has a hard black seed inside and juicy green flesh.

TRADITIONAL USES

Aboriginal People in the Kimberley consider Garlay a treasure and spend hours collecting the fruit, filling many buckets. Some people crush the flesh of the plums and create a paste to eat without the hard, black seeds getting in the way. Others prefer to eat them whole.

OTHER USES

This green plum is a delicious sweet and tangy treat on a hot day. Rich in vitamin C and fibre, it boosts your immune system and can be used to treat constipation.

KAKADU PLUM

ABORIGINAL NAME/S

Gubinge or kabiny plums – Bardi tribe, West Kimberley, Western Australia
Mudoorr – Jawi tribe, West Kimberley, Western Australia

BOTANICAL NAME

Terminalia ferndinandiana

Also known as billygoat plum or Murunga, the Kakadu plum tree is native to the tropical woodlands from north-western to eastern Arnhem Land, in the Northern Territory. It also grows in the east and west Kimberley regions, in Western Australia. A mature tree grows to 15m high, and has creamy grey bark and large oval-shaped leaves.

Between September and December, small creamy white flowers grow along the stems and produce a sweet aroma. The tree fruits from March to June.

The plums are sometimes light yellow but mostly light green, and around 10–20 grow on one long stem. They are an interesting shape – similar to an almond, about 2cm long and 1cm wide, with a pointy end.

TRADITIONAL USES

The Bardi People from the Dampier Peninsula, near Broome in Western Australia, use every part of the Mudoorr tree, learning from their ancestors not to waste anything. From December to May, just after the wet season, the local Aboriginal People are still harvesting the fruit. They not only eat the fruit, but they also eat the tree's sap by cooking it in a bowl over hot coals until it hardens.

The bark is also used as bush medicine, by boiling it and applying the liquid to the skin to heal rashes, infected sores and sunburn. This liquid is also drunk as a tea to treat inflammation in the joints.

OTHER USES

Kakadu plums have a sweet-and-sour flavour similar to dried apricots. They can be eaten raw and used in fruit salad.

They have also become extremely popular with health-food companies, because they contain antibacterial, antiviral and antifungal properties.

DID YOU KNOW?

Kakadu plums have the highest concentration of vitamin C of any fruit tested in the world. An orange contains 53mg of vitamin C, but a Kakadu plum contains an average of 2907mg!

LEMON ASPEN

ABORIGINAL NAME/S

Unknown

BOTANICAL NAME

Acronychia acidula

Lemon aspen can be found in north-eastern Queensland, from Cooktown to Mackay, but it can also be grown much further south. It will grow in both full sun and semi-shade, although it prefers well-drained soil with a sunny aspect and extra moisture when young.

This tree grows up to 2m high and has dark-green oval-shaped leaves. Its delicate white flowers smell sweet and appear in summer to late autumn, but last only a few weeks.

The small, cherry-sized fruit is about 1.5–2.5cm in diameter. It is a pale-lemon colour, and has a tough star-shaped core, similar to an apple, with small black seeds. The thin layer of flesh is slightly spongy. The fruit has an incredible tropical-citrus aroma and a sharp, lemony flavour. It needs to be picked when slightly underripe.

TRADITIONAL USES

Aboriginal People eat lemon aspen straight off the tree, and will also squash handfuls of the juice into a container. They drink the juice to boost the immune system and clear sore throats, and also use it as an antiseptic by rubbing it on sores or boils.

OTHER USES

Lemon aspen works best in dressings, marinades and dishes where a little can be added for a burst of freshness.

There are so many ways to use this versatile fruit, including in jams, jellies and juice. The whole fruit or just the juice can be used in pastries, desserts and sauces. The pulp from juicing can also flavour shortbread, mayonnaise or vinegar.

The leaves can also be used for flavouring. They are excellent in curds and salad dressings.

DID YOU KNOW?

The flavour of lemon aspen is extremely strong – just 100g of lemon aspen is equivalent to the juice, zest *and* pulp of about six large lemons!

LEMON MYRTLE

ABORIGINAL NAME/S

Djulungunu – Djabugay tribe, Kuranda, Far North Queensland

BOTANICAL NAME

Backhousia citriodora

Lemon myrtle grows in the cool, wet climate around northern and southern Queensland, and northern New South Wales, but sadly it does not grow in the wild anymore.

A healthy shrub will reach 1–5m high and 1.5m wide. It is attractive and lush, with full branches that hang gracefully. Long, thin leaves grow heavily on each branch, creating that full, bursting appeal.

In autumn the shrub grows stunning clusters of creamy-white flowers that give off an intensely sweet lemon fragrance. Lemon myrtle does not bear fruit – the leaves are the hero of this plant.

TRADITIONAL USES

Aboriginal People suck on the leaves to keep hydrated. This also provides them with nutrients, vitamins and minerals, which fight off diseases and give them energy. They also chew them or crush them into a paste to rub on sores or boils. The leaves can also be used as an insect repellent by burning them to create a thick smoke, which keeps the mosquitos away.

OTHER USES

In cooking, lemon myrtle leaves can be used in a similar way to bay leaves in marinades, soups, stews, casseroles and roasts. For desserts, try using dried, crushed leaves in cheesecake fillings or bases, apple crumble toppings, biscuits or cakes.

The plant contains anti-inflammatory properties, and sucking on the leaves to release their natural oils can treat swollen fingers, toes and joints.

To drink lemon myrtle as a tea, pluck a handful of leaves and add to a pot of boiling water, then wait until the water and the leaves turn slightly brown. This tea can be drunk warm or cold, and you can add a teaspoon of honey for extra flavour.

MACADAMIA

ABORIGINAL NAME/S

Boombera – Gumburra – Yugambeh Nation, South East Queensland and the Northern Rivers of New South Wales

BOTANICAL NAME

Macadamia integrifolia and *Macadamia tetraphylla*

This tree belongs to the genus *Macadamia*, which includes four species grown for their edible seeds or nuts. Macadamias can reach 20m high and 15m wide, with dark-green glossy leaves that are leathery in texture. These long, oval-shaped leaves have slight waves throughout, depending on the variety, and grow 20–30cm long with a spine running through the centre.

In spring, the tree produces cream, white and pinkish flowers. They grow in tight clusters that dangle from the branches. Each flower has five petals and a stem growing out of the centre.

After flowering, the tree produces the most incredible green, thick, leathery husks, which are formed in bunches of up to 20 fruits. Around February to April, the fruits will start to split to reveal the nuts. These nuts are round and up to 27mm in diameter and will fall to the ground when they are ripe. When the case is glossy brown, it's ready to eat!

You have to work hard to crack open the case and get to the delicious creamy nut. Once you do, you will find the flesh sits perfectly protected inside its casing.

TRADITIONAL USES

Traditionally, Aboriginal People harvested lots of macadamia nuts, as they were a great source of energy and protein, and keep your belly full.

The hard layer of the shell is also used for jewellery, and its sharp edges make a good cutting tool.

OTHER USES

These expensive nuts are mostly used in sweet dishes such as ice-creams, biscuits and cakes.

MIDYIM BERRY

ABORIGINAL NAME/S

Midyim – Kabi Kabi Nation

BOTANICAL NAME

Austromyrtus dulcis

Midyim berry, also known as sand berry, is a hardy plant. This unique-looking berry is an absolute favourite for many Aboriginal People, as it has a sweet taste with a slight hint of eucalyptus. Midyim berries are closely related to lilly pillies, and the shrubs mostly grow on the east coast of Australia, northern to southern parts of Queensland and as far south as central New South Wales.

The long needle-like leaves remind me of rosemary, but they are more spread out. They are spindly-shaped and a vibrant green colour, and grow 2–4cm long and 1–3mm wide. When young, the leaves are a maroon colour, then turn dark green with age.

Midyim flowers are white and delicate-looking, with five oval-shaped petals that grow 7–10mm wide. They are usually grouped in tight clusters on short stalks among the leafy foliage. In the midyim's natural habitat, these flowers appear in spring.

The midyim starts to fruit in summer. The berries are round, light purple and dotted with tiny dark-purple spots, and hold up to 10 pale-brown seeds.

TRADITIONAL USES

Some Kabi Kabi Elders have described these berries as their sweet treats, and people use them to make jams and pies. But I don't know how anyone gets them back to their kitchen – they are too scrumptious not to eat while harvesting!

Have fun with these berries and experiment! You can make jams or add them to smoothies, or even use them instead of blueberries in muffins.

Midyim berries are still a treat for Aboriginal People. The sweet, cinnamon-flavoured berries offer a high amount of vitamin C, antioxidants and fibre. Traditionally, the berries were mainly eaten by women and children.

MOUNTAIN BUSH PEPPER BERRY

ABORIGINAL NAME/S

Tapu – Palawa Kani, Tasmania

BOTANICAL NAME

Tasmannia lanceolata

This versatile bush treasure grows naturally in cool, wet rainforest areas around Tasmania, southern New South Wales, and throughout Victoria. It is a small tree that grows 3–8m high and 1–2m wide, with attractive bright-red stems and glossy dark-green leaves.

It produces cream-coloured flowers from October to January, depending on its location. The berry-like fruits are 5–10mm in diameter, beginning dark red and turning shiny black when ripe in summer or autumn. The berries generally appear only on female trees, though plants of both sexes contain flowers.

TRADITIONAL USES

Traditionally, mountain bush pepper was eaten to treat infections. Sore gums and toothaches can be treated by crushing the berries into a paste with a bit of water and applying it to the affected areas. This paste has a sting to it, but it kills the bacteria in the infection.

OTHER USES

Mountain bush pepper has a strong earthy flavour with a hint of heat. You can add ground leaves to olive oil for dressings. The berries add a unique flavour to dukkah, and roasted meats or vegetables. You can also 'pinch' it over soups and sauces, much like black pepper.

OLD MAN SALTBUSH

ABORIGINAL NAME/S

Purngep, pining and binga – Noongar tribe, Western Australia

BOTANICAL NAME

Atriplex nummularia

This silver-grey shrub grows to 1–3m tall and 2–5m wide. It is popular in gardens as hedging or screening as the colour contrasts nicely against other green plants.

Old man saltbush grows in all parts of Australia, in arid to subtropical environments with cool to warm temperatures. It is resistant to drought and sandy soil, but in the wild, young plants struggle in conditions that are too dry and barren.

The leaves are rough, with a scaly coating and crinkled edges. The small flowers are either male or female, and grow on different plants. The female flowers grow in dense clusters, approximately 20cm long, while the male flowers are globe-shaped and crowd along the end of each branch.

Saltbush will grow well in the ground, or in small pots if you harvest it often. It's a great way to fill space in garden beds, but it will need to be pruned as it sprawls! The great thing about this plant is that you can harvest the leaves all year to use in all kinds of cooking. The leaves and seeds add a rich salty flavour, as well as antioxidants and protein, to every dish.

TRADITIONAL USES

Saltbush is used by Aboriginal People to treat wounds, sores and burns. It is crushed up into a paste with water and applied to the infected area.

OTHER USES

You can use old man saltbush just as you would salt and pepper. Adding this native herb to one or two of your dishes will not only make your food taste delicious, but is a great way to create a unique and memorable dish. It's perfect for giving a strong, salty flavour to salads and savoury dishes.

PIGFACE

ABORIGINAL NAME/S

Karkalla, bain – Noongar tribe, Western Australia
Janga – Wajarri tribe, Western Australia
Pigface kanikung/canajong – Palawa tribe, Tasmania

BOTANICAL NAME

Carpobrotus rossii

I know what you're thinking: it's a weird name for a bush fruit! Well, the name pigface comes from two things: some say the fruit resembles a pig's face, and others say the fruits are in the shape of a pig. But please don't let the name deter you!

Also known as noon flower, ice plant and cutwort, it is native to South Africa and Australia. It grows in Queensland, New South Wales, Western Australia, South Australia, Tasmania and Victoria, and can be seen year-round in large patches along coastline areas. It grows low to the ground, up to 1m high, but can spread as wide as 3m.

Bright-pink flowers bloom in August to October, and continue through summer. The succulent blue-green leaves are long, plump, firm and triangle-shaped. Poking up from the soil, they have a clear jelly-like texture inside.

The fruit ripens when the flower is pollinated, and remains on the stem after the flower dries up and falls off. The fig-like fruits turn a deep pink to red colour, and are the size of red grapes.

The pigface fruit has a delicious salty but sweet flavour. Just hold one end and suck out the sweet pulp, or eat it whole. The flesh is soft and gooey with a large number of small seeds, similar to a dragon fruit. It also has a delicious salty skin!

TRADITIONAL USES

Many Aboriginal People eat the fruit fresh or sun-dried, and the salty leaves are roasted on hot coals and eaten with meat. The juice of the succulent leaves is used to treat sores, infections and burns, very similar to how aloe vera leaves are used.

OTHER USES

This plant is used to make gourmet jams, chutneys, jellies and cakes, or is paired with seafood in savoury dishes.

DID YOU KNOW?

Pigface can be used to keep hydrated if fresh water isn't available.

RAINFOREST TAMARIND

ABORIGINAL NAME/S

Biliybiliy – Djabugay tribe, Kuranda, Far North Queensland

BOTANICAL NAME

Diploglottis smithii

These tall, thin trees grow up to 20m high, and are native to South East Queensland and northern New South Wales. They grow in wet, tropical rainforests, and can be found along coastal lowland around northern New South Wales, on the Sunshine Coast, and away from the coast and in the highlands in parts of Queensland.

The large, rounded green leaves are almost leathery or waxy-looking, and the small, delicate, creamy flowers bloom in summer.

The fruit grows in clusters, and is ready to harvest in autumn. It hangs gracefully in a light-brown casing holding three vibrant red seeds. The flesh is sour and tangy – similar to green mango.

TRADITIONAL USES

Aboriginal People gather native tamarinds every year. Eaten raw, the fruits are a delicious treat.

Traditionally, women and children would sit by a river or creek and crush the fruit off the seeds. Then they would add water to create a refreshing beverage.

OTHER USES

Native tamarind can be made into jams, chutneys and sauces for savoury, sour and sweet dishes. The tangy, sour flavour can also work well in baked dishes such as cheesecakes, biscuits and slices. It also makes refreshing cordial.

Native tamarind is full of vitamin C and natural minerals, making it a great way to boost your immune system.

SANDPAPER FIG

ABORIGINAL NAME/S

Yanggi – Djabugay tribe, Kuranda, Far North Queensland

BOTANICAL NAME

Ficus fraseri

Sandpaper fig trees are often seen as a weed, but these hardy trees are an important part of the ecosystem, providing food for birds, caterpillars, butterflies, fruit bats, flying foxes and many other animals.

Sandpaper figs grow well in warm, dry climates around water systems, riverbanks, rainforests and creeks. They are found in the northern parts of Australia and along the east coast, from Mackay in Queensland through New South Wales and just into Victoria near Mallacoota. A mature tree can reach about 8m in height, but along coastal edges the trees grow much smaller (about 2–4m), due to the high winds.

The name 'sandpaper fig' comes from the texture of the leaves, which are rough and harsh – exactly like sandpaper. These dark-green leaves grow 5–15cm long.

The tree flowers and fruits from spring to early summer, and the fruit matures from December to February. The fruits are small and round. They go from green to deep maroon when ripe, and grow 1–2cm. They are sweet and moist, with hundreds of little brown seeds. Like common figs, the outer layer is soft and sweet, and the tiny hairs are fine to eat.

TRADITIONAL USES

Traditionally, the tree was more than just a food source. The men used the leaves to sand down tools and weapons – such as boomerangs, spears, coolamons (wooden bowls) and axe handles – to a smooth surface. And the thick white tree sap was, and still is, used to treat the itchy symptoms and skin infections of ringworm by applying a thin layer over the ringworm scars.

OTHER USES

Sandpaper figs are sometimes found on menus in restaurants, cooked in the same way as common figs, either roasted, baked or pan-fried.

WATTLESEED

ABORIGINAL NAME/S

Merne ntange arlepe – Arrernte tribe, central Australia, Northern Territory

BOTANICAL NAME

Acacia

As there are so many species and forms of acacia, they have been a mainstay in the diet of Aboriginal Australians for thousands of years. Please note, however, that not all acacias are suitable for humans to eat – some contain high levels of toxins. Always make sure you only gather wattleseed with a knowledgeable adult.

Shrubby-looking wattle trees grow as tall as 6m. The branches are spindly and covered with spiky thorns up to 1cm long, and slender light-green leaves 4–8cm long.

Wattles prefer hot, dry temperatures. The seeds are encased in hard husks, and will last up to 20 years in their natural environment, usually only germinating after bushfires.

They flower in August through to December, depending on the region. Each stem holds up to 12 flower clusters, which first appear pale before changing to a vibrant yellow. The seeds are best collected when they are dry and turn dark brown, generally from January to March.

TRADITIONAL USES

For thousands of years, Aboriginal People have eaten the green seeds raw, or dried and milled them into flour for baking. Since the hard outer casing protects the seed for so long on the ground, wattleseed is an especially good food in times of drought. And, although the plant is a member of the traditionally poisonous *Acacia* genus, Aboriginal People have discovered more than 40 different edible varieties!

The seeds can then be ground into a paste and mixed with water to form small, flat cakes that are baked in the coals of a fire, then eaten or stored for later use.

OTHER USES

Wattleseed is the unsung hero of Australian native foods! It is high in protein and contains potassium, calcium, iron and zinc. It can be dried and roasted in a similar way to coffee, then ground and crushed into a powder for use in cooking.

The flavour is a bit like hazelnut and chocolate with hints of coffee. This makes it an ideal seasoning for ice-creams, nutty flavoured butters, sauces and coffee.

ANIMALS

SOOTY GRUNTER

ABORIGINAL NAME/S

Wulam – Djabugay tribe, Kuranda, Far North Queensland

SCIENTIFIC NAME

Hephaestus fuliginosus

Sooty grunters, also known as black bream, are a common fish, related to (but not to be mistaken for!) saltwater sea bream. They are golden-brown when in the water, but their scales turn black out of the water – that's why they are called black bream. On average they grow to 60cm long and weigh 4kg.

You can catch them mainly in rivers, creeks and billabongs. They prefer to swim under overhanging branches, among the branches of fallen trees, and in the bottom of deep waterholes.

In summer and early autumn, young and adult bream can be found in the upper level of the estuaries, but they often get washed downstream when the first rains fall.

They are usually found around the northern part of Australia, from Kimberley Region of Western Australia, Northern Territory across Arnhem Land, East Coast of Queensland, Cape York and Omnivorous of Carpentaria. Their spawning period occurs in summer after the water temperatures reaches 25°C and the water level rises.

Sooty grunters are omnivorous and eat a wide variety of food, including prawns, worms, insects, frogs, algae, plant root and palm berries.

TRADITIONAL USES

Small and easy to catch, black bream is a treat among Aboriginal People. It's often caught and cooked straight out of the water (with scales and guts, so nothing gets wasted) or by putting it on the coals for 5–10 minutes. Once it's cooked, the skin is peeled off to reveal the white, steaming-hot flesh. It tastes slightly sweet, and is a healthy source of protein.

BUSTARD BIRD

ABORIGINAL NAME/S

Wawun – Djabugay tribe, Kuranda, Far North Queensland

SCIENTIFIC NAME

Ardeotis australis

Known to Aboriginal People as bush turkey or plain turkey (but, importantly, not to be confused with *brush* turkeys!), these large ground birds roam grasslands, woodlands and open plains across the northern and central parts of Australia, where it is warm and dry.

The bustard bird can grow as tall as 1.5m, and has a wingspan of 2.5m – that's even wider than a queen-size bed! An average male can weigh 6.5kg, but the female birds are smaller and more slender. A bustard bird's body is mostly dull brown, with black and white speckles on its wings. Its head is crowned with black feathers, while its neck and the bottom half of its body is grey – this helps it to blend in with its surroundings.

TRADITIONAL USES

Bush turkeys play an important role in the diet of Aboriginal People throughout the Kimberley, the central desert and Far North Queensland. They are still eaten today, but are protected in some parts of Australia, although Aboriginal People are still allowed to hunt them.

They also play an important part in the Dreaming stories, and are a spiritual totem for many Aboriginal People.

Traditionally, Aboriginal men hunted bush turkeys using a spear with a woomera, which allowed the spear to be thrown faster, further, harder and more accurately. When the men brought a bush turkey back to camp, the women and children were responsible for preparing it by plucking all the feathers off, then burning off all the baby feathers. Then they would cut it open and remove the organs, keeping all the best bits, such as the gizzards, heart, kidney and liver. It was then cooked on the hot coals, which kept the protein and the healthy fats and oils in the flesh.

COMMON LONG-NECKED TURTLE

ABORIGINAL NAME/S

Min bungarra – Kokoberra tribe, Kowanyama, Cape York Region, Far North Queensland

SCIENTIFIC NAME

Chelodina rugosa

This turtle's neck can grow up to 30cm long, and is sometimes longer than the body! Its feet are webbed and very strong, and it often uses its feet to tear apart its food. It also has a sharp beak and strong jaw, so make sure you keep your fingers away from its beak!

Its dark brown colouring helps it to hide from predators around rocks and mud. It also buries itself in mudflats or dried-up riverbeds for protection during the dry season.

Like other reptiles, common long-necked turtles are most active during the dry season, travelling long distances in search of new waterholes. During winter, they lie dormant under logs and rocks, waiting for the water temperature to change before they go in search of food.

In the Kimberley region, another species of long-necked turtle can be found. The Kimberley snake-necked turtle has very long chin barbels – thin, thread-like fibres that hang from the bottom of its chin. This is where its tastebuds are located, helping the turtle search for food in murky waters.

TRADITIONAL USES

Aboriginal People enjoy eating turtle and often prefer it to fish.

When the people in Arnhem Land hunt snake-necked turtles, they go to the cracked mudflats and walk along until they see a minuscule bubble among the hard, brown mud – a clue that there's a turtle in the damp mud underneath, keeping moist and cool away from the sun!

Aboriginal People will often cook a turtle with the shell facing down on the hot coals. They do not gut the turtle before cooking it. When holes appear around the legs and the shell, the flesh inside is cooked.

There are a few ways to crack open the shell. One is to crack it with a hard object, like a hammer or rock. Another is to cut the breast plate away from the shell, exposing the legs and guts, and keeping the juices in the shell.

Traditionally, turtle fats were rubbed onto the chest of sick or weak babies to give them strength. Today, It is still practised that whenever you catch a turtle, you must give it to the old people first as a sign of respect.

COORONG COCKLE

ABORIGINAL NAME/S

Bulkiji – Kuku Yalanji tribe, Far North Queensland

SCIENTIFIC NAME

Plebidonax deltoides or *Donax deltoides*

Also called Goolwa cockle or Goolwa pipi, these shellfish are most commonly known simply as pipis or clams. They can be found on beaches throughout the eastern parts of Australia, and also in New Zealand.

Pipis have a strong shell that measures up to 6cm and is a distinctive wedged shape, with the front edge rounded and the rear side straight. The outside of the shell varies in colour from a beautiful violet to pink, yellow, brown and green. The inside is generally white with purple or pink colouring.

Pipis are harvested both to be eaten and to be used as bait. Eaten raw, straight out of the shell, pipi meat is sweet, salty and rubbery. It has a gritty texture due to the sand the pipis absorb from the sea floor. The best way to eat pipis is to first soak them in salt water to keep them alive, then rinse them in fresh water so they can spit out the sand.

Pipis can be found on low tide – when the waves wash away, lumps are exposed on the sandy beach. Pipis burrow just beneath the surface of the sand, and just below the water level on the beach. They can quickly bury themselves again if washed around by the surf.

TRADITIONAL USES

Pipis are enjoyed raw or cooked on hot coals until their shells open up. Traditionally, the shells were used as knives to cut up soft foods, or to make jewellery, such as headdresses, necklaces and belts.

There is evidence that pipis have been an important part of the diet of coastal saltwater people for a long time. Pipi middens (collections of discarded shells) have been found deep in the sand dunes in northern New South Wales, Queensland, Arnhem land and the Kimberleys.

OTHER USES

Pipis are a delicacy in the culinary world, and are in high demand in restaurants!

CROCODILE

ABORIGINAL NAME/S

Baru – many language groups of Arnhem Land, Northern Territory

SCIENTIFIC NAME

Crocodylus porosus (saltwater), *Crocodylus johnstoni* (freshwater)

In Australia we have two species of crocodiles, freshwater and saltwater. Freshwater crocodiles are smaller with a narrow snout. They are light brown, with dark markings on the body and tail, and generally live in freshwater habitats, in the warmer waters of the northern parts of Australia. They feed mainly on fish and smaller vertebrates.

Saltwater species are more aggressive, and are the largest living reptiles. They have a wider head and a broad, rounded snout.

When young, they are pale yellow and light brown, then become dark green as an adult.

Don't be fooled by the name *saltwater* crocodile, either. These giant reptiles can survive in both fresh and salt water! The male can grow up to 7m long (longer than a car!) and weigh up to 2000kg, but the female generally reaches only 3m long. They live in mangrove swamps, lagoons, estuaries and low stretches of rivers throughout the northern parts of Western Australia, the Northern Territory, the Gulf of Carpentaria and Queensland.

Saltwater crocodiles will eat almost anything – fish, turtles, wild pigs, wallabies, kangaroos, buffalos, dingos, live cattle, dogs and even humans. So, when you're taking a swim or strolling along the far northern beaches or rivers in Australia, beware and abide by the signage!

OTHER USES

Crocodile meat is an increasingly popular bush food, and is farmed and sold by butchers. Low in fat, high in protein and surprisingly tasty and tender, this white meat is featured on restaurant menus around the world. It can be used in curries, stir-fries, stews, sausages, pies and casseroles.

ECHIDNA

ABORIGINAL NAME/S

Inape/inarlenge – eastern and central Arrernte language groups, Northern Territory
Tjilkamata – Arrernte People of Central Australia

SCIENTIFIC NAME

Tachyglossus aculeatus

Echidnas are 30–45cm long and can weigh 2–7kg. These egg-laying mammals are covered with long, coarse black hair and sharp, black-tipped needles. They have a stubby, hairless tail and long, sharp-clawed feet, which they use to burrow through the ground, fossicking for food and water. They also find food – ants or other insects – with their long, sensitive nose, then use their long, slim, sticky tongue to catch it.

Echidnas are always found roaming on their own. They can be found throughout most of Australia, especially around rocks, hollow logs, termite mounds and holes around tree roots.

TRADITIONAL USES

The Arrernte People of central Australia still hunt echidna today. Echidnas are fast on their feet and are fast diggers, so in order to capture one you have to quickly roll it onto its back so it can't run away.

Before Aboriginal People cook echidna, they carefully gut it to remove its poisonous sack, then close up the hole with a skewer. To remove the needles, they boil the echidna, then hold it in place with a strong wire looped around its feet while scraping off the needles with a small axe or sharp knife. Once the needles are removed, the echidna is placed on the fire to burn off the remaining coarse hair, before being placed into a camp oven for 2–3 hours, until the meat is cooked right through and bubbling with juices.

OTHER USES

To some it might seem cruel to eat cute little echidnas – but this animal has been a staple of Aboriginal People's diet for thousands of years, and is still eaten today. It is a protected species in some states.

EMU

ABORIGINAL NAME/S

Karnanganyjal – Jaru tribe, Western Desert, East Kimberley, Western Australia

SCIENTIFIC NAME

Dromaius novaehollandiae

This flightless bird stands 2m high – that's taller than an average man. The emu is the second-largest living bird in the world. It is found over most of mainland Australia, and prefers to roam dry savannah, bushy or scrubby woodlands, and dry areas.

Emus have long, thin necks and soft brown and grey waterproof feathers. They have light-blue skin around their necks, and red eyes. Their strong, leathery feet have three toes and long, strong black nails, which are one of their only ways to defend themselves. Their long legs allow them to take strides of up to 2.75m, making them extremely fast runners – they are able to sprint at 50km per hour!

Emus breed in May and June, and a female can mate with several males and lay several batches of eggs in one season. The eggs hatch after about eight weeks, and the young chicks are looked after by their fathers. An emu can live for up to 20 years.

TRADITIONAL USES

Among Aboriginal People, emus are well respected as they represent totems and skin names, and are spiritually important. Skin names are a kinship, which means everyone is given a skin name to identify who they are related to.

The Yuwaalaraay and other clans around New South Wales say that the spirits created the sun by throwing an emu egg into the sky. The emu is also believed to lie in the Milky Way, high in the sky, looking over many Aboriginal language groups.

In most tribes, the emu is also important for its meat and feathers, which were traded with other groups. Traditionally, the men hunted emus. They imitated the emu's mating calls, covered themselves in emu feathers and used their arms as the neck to lure male emus closer before striking them with a spear or axe.

Emu fat is good for the skin as a moisturiser, giving it a nice shine, but it also helps relieve aching bones and joints.

OTHER USES

Emu meat is high in protein and low in fat. It is dark red and best fried or cooked on a hot plate, like a barbecue.

REPTILE

FILE SNAKE

ABORIGINAL NAME/S

Kedjebe – Kunwinjku tribe, western Arnhem Land, Northern Territory

SCIENTIFIC NAME

Acrochordus arafurae

Also known as the elephant trunk snake, Arafura file snake or wrinkle file snake, this non-venomous water snake is mostly found in freshwater swamps, creeks and billabongs in Arnhem Land in the Northern Territory. You can identify file snakes quite easily as they are light to dark brown with a very thick body and a small, bulldog-shaped head. The females are larger than the males, and can grow as long as 2.5m and weigh about 1.5kg.

File snakes get their name from the rough, spiky, scaly, file-like texture of their skin. They mostly breed in the dry season, and the females only breed once every few years. If the eggs survive attacks from crocodiles and birds, they give birth to approximately 20–30 babies.

TRADITIONAL USES

In the far north Arnhem Land region, Aboriginal women and children often hunt for file snakes. These docile water snakes rest in the mud, in slow water or even on riverbanks. The women and children walk through crocodile-infested waters, using their feet to feel around in the mud. When they feel something scaly, they bend down and grab the file snake, and reach for its head to kill it instantly. They cook it whole on hot coals for 15–20 minutes. The flesh is white, with a sweet flavour and a stringy texture – it's very similar to chicken, but is fattier.

Yolŋu People in north-east Arnhem Land have a spiritual connection to the file snake as an ancient totem. It often appears in their artwork and stories as the rainbow serpent and lightning spirit: creator of the waterholes, rivers, hills, valleys and mountains.

OTHER USES

Some people find it hard to gather the courage to eat snake, but file snake is high in protein and healthy oils. And best of all, it tastes delicious!

FRESHWATER MUD MUSSEL

ABORIGINAL NAME/S

Ngidjubany or gudjubay – Djabugay tribe, Kuranda, Far North Queensland

SCIENTIFIC NAME

Velesunio wilsonii

Freshwater mud mussels prefer warmer climates can be found in the muddy banks of billabongs, rivers, creeks and lakes. Like common green mussels, they grow in black, ear-shaped shells. An adult mussel can grow up to 12cm long. The shell's markings are similar to the rings in a tree's trunk, and the top and bottom are joined by two very strong white hinges.

Inside, the shell is pearly white and has a pretty, lustrous sheen – it is sometimes called pearl-shell. It holds the soft, rubbery mussel, which is said to be not as tasty as its saltwater relative. These mussels are very sensitive to pollution.

TRADITIONAL USES

Traditionally, freshwater mud mussels were an important source of food for Aboriginal People. Women and girls would search for them while the men watched for crocodiles. The women and girls would immerse themselves in the water of creeks or rivers, and swim along the banks, using their hands to dig around the muddy banks for mussels. They would fill their woven dilly bags, coolamons or paperbark baskets with them.

The flesh was eaten after roasting in hot coals or boiling in water. Freshwater mud mussels were one of the foods Aboriginal People ate when they were in mourning.

The shells were also used as tools for carving or cutting.

GOANNA

ABORIGINAL NAME/S

Barni – Bardi tribe, West Kimberley, Western Australia
Ganyal – Djabugay tribe, Kuranda, Far North Queensland

SCIENTIFIC NAME

Varanus

There are 30 species of goanna in the world, and 25 are found in Australia. Goannas (also called Australian monitors) are giant carnivorous lizards with sharp teeth and claws. They can grow as big as 3m long, and prey on birds, bird eggs and small mammals. They are mostly dark in colouring, with camouflage tones of cream, grey, black, brown and green.

These reptiles are found all over Australia, mostly in warmer climates. They live underground in burrows or in hollow logs, but with their sharp claws can also climb tall trees to get away from predators and hunt for baby birds or eggs.

TRADITIONAL USE

Goannas are a delicacy among Aboriginal People. They feature strongly in Dreaming stories and as individual, family and clan spiritual totems. People who have an animal as a spiritual totem are responsible for the protection of that animal so it doesn't get over-hunted, and the spiritual stories attached to it are maintained.

It takes a lot of skill and energy to hunt a goanna. After tracking the lizard to find its burrow, you then have to flush it out to catch it – but goannas are extremely quick, so if you miss it, you'll have to be a very fast runner to chase it down. Most of the time, it'll run for the nearest tree, hollow log or burrow.

To cook goanna, Aboriginal People make a fire, then throw it on the flames to burn off the tough layer of skin. They then let the fire burn down, dig a hole in the middle of the hot coals, place the goanna inside and cover it with the hot coals for 30–40 minutes.

The best parts of the goanna to eat are the legs and the tail. The meat is white, and tastes like chicken breast, but is a little drier. It is best eaten with the fat, which takes the experience to a whole other level, making the meat moist and rich! Aboriginal People regard fat as the prize of the animal, because it gives you energy.

OTHER USES

Goanna oil is an important bush medicine within Aboriginal communities. It is rubbed on the skin as a natural moisturiser and to treat aching muscles and joints.

GRASSHOPPER

ABORIGINAL NAME/S

Muurruung – Wiradjuri tribe, Central New South Wales

SCIENTIFIC NAME

Orthoptera Caelifera

These insects can be found all over Australia. They have two pairs of narrow, transparent wings and two big hind legs for jumping, each with sharp defensive spikes. They also have short antennae, large eyes and two front and middle legs for balance.

Grasshoppers come out mainly in spring and summer, but they are most noticeable in autumn, when they gather in groups, or swarms, causing plagues.

TRADITIONAL USES

Just after the wet season, when there are lots of grasshoppers around, they are easy to catch. Traditionally, women and children have fun doing this.

Aboriginal People eat grasshoppers by crisping them up on hot coals. They are crunchy with a nutty flavour, and are full of protein. They also make great bait when fishing for both fish and turtles.

OTHER USES

Another way to cook grasshoppers is to collect 5–10 large ones, remove the legs and stir-fry them in hot oil with garlic and light soy sauce. They are really tasty!

DID YOU KNOW?

There are about 500 native grasshopper species in Australia, and over 8000 species around the world!

GREEN ANT

ABORIGINAL NAME/S

Djiliburay – Djabugay tribe, Kuranda, Far North Queensland

SCIENTIFIC NAME

Oecophylla smaragdina

Also known as weaver ants, green ants are found throughout northern Australia and South East Queensland, in the open woodland and rainforests. Green ants crawl over everything, but can be seen in trees, building their nest by weaving and gluing leaves together.

These ants pack a punch if you're bitten, but they will only bite if they feel threatened or scared. Their bodies are yellow, and they have six thin legs and two antennae, which are as long as their middle and back legs. They get their name from their green abdomens.

TRADITIONAL USES

Aboriginal People swear by the medicinal properties of green ants. They eat the ants individually by picking one up between their fingertips and biting off the green abdomen, then releasing the ant – it has a tangy citrus flavour, and the green abdomen can help stomach aches, sore throats, and other cold and flu symptoms.

The ants can also be squished between the hands and inhaled to clear the sinuses – but the trick is to not get bitten! The best way to do this is to carefully grab the ant by the head. If more ants climb on your arms, try not to panic – just flick them off gently.

To get a stronger effect, an entire nest can be boiled in hot water for 10 minutes. Then, once the liquid is cooled, it is drained through a clean cloth, straining out the ants, which are then squeezed to get out any remaining juice. Aboriginal People use the liquid to treat sore throats, aching bones and headaches by pouring it over their heads or drinking it. They also add honey to sweeten it, as the mixture has a tangy, bitter flavour.

OTHER USES

Green ants are the most valued insect eaten by humans, looked upon as a delicacy in countries like Thailand and Indonesia.

INSECT

HONEY ANT

ABORIGINAL NAME/S

Agkwarle yerrampe or tjupi/tjala – Arrernte, Luritja and Pitjantjatjara tribes, Central Australia, Northern Territory
Yarumpa – Kaytetye tribe

SCIENTIFIC NAME

Camponotus inflatus

While honeybees collect and store their liquids in a nest or in a comb, honey ants are unique as they store liquid in their own bodies. They start off looking like normal ants. Worker ants feed nectar to the honey ants, which is converted into honey and stored in their abdomens. This then grows into a 'honey pot'.

Honey ants are predominantly found in the hot, dry, arid terrains of the desert regions of Australia, where they live deep underground. Trapped by their pea-sized abdomen, they are unable to reach the surface, but they serve as living larders for other ants.

A honey ant has a red head, black body and six legs; the honey pot is round and golden, with two thick black bands on the back.

TRADITIONAL USES

Aboriginal People from central Australia call honey ants 'Ngkwarle yerrampe', which means 'honey ant Dreaming'. Aboriginal women will look for a small hole on the ground, which indicates the entrance of the nest below. They then dig into the ant colony. They have to be gentle and patient because sometimes the nests are buried deep in the ground.

Once they find the nest, they carefully pluck the honey ants out to collect and distribute them among the other women and children. They only eat the back of the ant – the honey pot – and then they place the ant back in the nest. It's hard work, but very rewarding.

Honey ants also play an important part in the Dreaming stories of the Warlpiri People.

OTHER USES

Honey ants are mostly used as a sweet treat that gives a burst of energy, but they are also good for sore throats. They contain antioxidants and have antiviral properties, which makes them a good medicine.

KANGAROO

ABORIGINAL NAME/S

Gangurru – Guugu Yimithir tribe, Far North Queensland

SCIENTIFIC NAME

Macropus rufus (red kangaroo), *Macropus giganteus* (eastern grey kangaroo), *Macropus fuliginosus* (western grey kangaroo), *Macropus antilopinus* (antilopine kangaroo)

The kangaroo is a marsupial with powerful hind legs, large feet for leaping and a long, muscular tail for balance. There are four different species of kangaroo found all over Australia. They don't live in any particular habitat – they are comfortable hopping all over the countryside, and can reach speeds of up to 70km per hour for nearly 2kms! They are nocturnal animals, so they need to rest during the day.

The red kangaroo is the largest, and is found mostly in the arid and semi-arid centre of Australia. A male can grow as tall as 2m, and weigh 90–100kg. The eastern grey kangaroo lives on the east coast of Australia, and the western grey kangaroo lives in the southern part of Australia. The antilopine kangaroo is found in the far northern parts of Australia, enjoying the grassy plains and woodlands.

TRADITIONAL USES

The word 'kangaroo' originated from the Guugu Yimithir word 'Gangurru', which was recorded in a diary entry by English botanist Joseph Banks as 'kanguru' in the 1770s.

Kangaroos play an important part in the Dreaming stories of many Aboriginal language groups across Australia, and are important spiritual totems for some tribes.

Traditionally, Aboriginal men were the hunters of larger animals, especially kangaroo, using weapons like the spear and woomera. As with most bush tukka, every part of the kangaroo was used – the meat, the fur and even the sinew, which was used to bind weapons and tools. Once the animal was killed, its blood would be drained and shared among the men and boys of the tribe so that they could take on its strength, speed and wisdom.

OTHER USES

Kangaroo meat is lean, high in protein, low in fat, rich in iron and full of flavour. It works well in all dishes and styles of cooking, from stir-fries, slow-cooked stews, curries and casseroles to kebabs, pasta sauce and roasts

MAGPIE GOOSE

ABORIGINAL NAME/S

Djawadjawa dagi – Djabugay tribe, Kuranda, Far North Queensland

SCIENTIFIC NAME

Anseranas semipalmata

A magpie goose is black from the top of its head to the base of its neck, with black wings. Its body is covered in white feathers, with orange legs and beak. It is a very noisy bird, making a deep honking sound to communicate to others!

These birds can be found around wetlands, swamps, floodplains and cane paddocks, but they regularly move around to different locations during the dry season. They live mostly around savannah and northern coastal parts of Australia, like the Kimberley regions in Western Australia, the Top End in the Northern Territory, and in Far North Queensland.

TRADITIONAL USE

The Ganalbingu, or Magpie Goose People, are the largest clan in central Arnhem Land. They have a respect for magpie geese and their spirit, as it is part of the Ganalbingu Dreaming. Magpie goose eggs and nests are sacred, as they are seen as the resting place for the geese's souls.

Aboriginal People of north central Arnhem Land cook magpie geese on hot coals. They put paperbark leaves on the coals and place the magpie geese on top. Then they cover it with more paperbark and sand until no steam comes out. After 40 minutes they dust off the sand and remove the paperbark sheets. Magpie geese have dark, rich flesh very similar to bustard meat (see page 52) but much more tender.

OTHER USES

Magpie geese are not widely known or used, but the Aboriginal People of Arnhem Land still hunt and eat them today.

MANGROVE SNAIL

ABORIGINAL NAME/S

Djidin or gudjubay – Djabugay tribe, Kuranda, Far North Queensland

SCIENTIFIC NAME

Nerita lineata

Also known as periwinkles, mangrove snails are 1–2 cm long, and can be found around rocky shores, reef rocks and mangrove vegetation, mostly in the northern regions of Australia. They often cluster together in large numbers near watermarks around mangrove roots.

Their shell is rounded and strong, usually black or grey, with distinguishing black stripes down the back. Underneath, it is smooth with a tinge of yellow at the outer entrance of the shell. The snail is pale with thin black bands on its single foot, and long, thin black tentacles that help it become aware of predators like birds, crabs or humans. When the snail senses danger, it retreats into its shell, which it seals off with a little door, or lid, to protect it against predators.

Mangrove snails are herbivores. They feed on algae growing on reef rocks and mangrove roots.

TRADITIONAL USES

Aboriginal People throughout regions in northern Australia enjoy collecting these snails from the mangroves and off the rocks by the ocean. They are best cooked on hot coals for 3–5 minutes, until liquid bubbles from the shell's entrance and the lid begins to pop open.

To access the snail, either crack the back of the shell or find a thin, sharp stick and peel the lid away, fishing out the snail at the same time. They can also be boiled in water for about 10 minutes.

OTHER USES

Mangrove snails offer the same delicacy as land snails, or *escargot*, which are served as appetisers in France. You can fry or bake these morsels in garlic-herb butter, just like *escargot*.

You can also use mangrove snails for bait, and they are particularly good for catching barramundi.

MUD CRAB

ABORIGINAL NAME/S

Ngudoong – Jawi tribe, West Kimberley, Western Australia

SCIENTIFIC NAME

Scylla serrata

Australia has two species of mud crabs: green mud crabs and brown mud crabs. A mature green mud crab can grow up to 30cm wide and weigh 2.5kg. The brown mud crab grows to half the size of a green mud crab: 15cm wide, and weighing 1.5kg.

They are abundant in estuaries, mangrove swamps, creeks and rivers, and in more protected environments like under mangrove roots, in mud and water pools.

Female crabs are protected. If you catch a jenny crab (as a female crab is called), you must release it back into the mud or water. You can easily tell a jenny crab by its abdominal flaps, which are triangle-shaped and much broader than the male or 'buck' abdominal flaps. Also, when female jenny crabs reach their mature cycle, their claws are a lot smaller than a male crab.

When catching mud crab by hand, be very careful! Their nippers can cut through almost anything, including your fingers. It is best to approach a mud crab from behind and hold its body down using a stick, then grab the back swimmer-legs in a firm lock. The nippers will rise to try to attack you, but they don't go backwards, so you can catch it without getting hurt.

TRADITIONAL USES

Aboriginal People have enjoyed mud crab hunting for thousands of years. They used to catch mud crabs by hand, or using a stick or spears to force them from their burrows. The traditional way to cook mud crabs is directly on hot coals, and every part of the mud crab is eaten. Nothing is wasted except the gills, which are too tough and bitter to eat. The best part is what Aboriginal People call 'the soup'. This is the guts of the crab – the yellow and white creamy substance you find under the main shell when you peel it open. The soup is rich in protein, vitamins and minerals, including zinc and iron. The claws are also very yummy.

OTHER USES

One of the most popular modern dishes is chilli mud crabs, which is from Singapore. Aboriginal People did not have chillies or sauces until recently, when they were introduced by pearl drivers who ventured over from Singapore, Malaysia and Japan in the early 1970s.

MUD WHELK

ABORIGINAL NAME/S

Damitjarra – Larrakia tribe, Northern Territory

SCIENTIFIC NAME

Telescopium telescopium

Mud whelks are also known as long bums! Mud whelks have long cone-shaped shells that are brown with a creamy spiral pattern. The shells have a large opening at the bottom of the cone, and can grow up to 11cm long. These shells sometimes house hermit crabs, so be careful when gathering and cooking them. You can tell that a mud whelk lives inside the shell by the colour inside – it should be light blue. The mud whelk itself is the most amazing bright blue colour.

They prefer the warm climates of Northern Australia, and can be found at low tide, living in muddy banks around mangrove vegetation and roots, and near watermarks. They are often clustered together in large numbers.

When you cook mud whelks on the hot coals, it's best to place them sharp end down, with the open end sticking out of the coals – this way, the whole snail will cook thoroughly.

To get the snail out of the shell, you need to poke it with a sharp metal object – but there is a trick to it, as the snail will break if you're not gentle. Another way is to get a hard object and break the side of the shell after it has been cooked. Then you can fish out the snail, splitting the body in half.

TRADITIONAL USES

Mud whelks are a delicacy among Aboriginal People, and are also eaten to fight viral and chest infections because of their rich mineral content.

OTHER USES

Mud whelks are not very widely used, as they are not seen as an attractive bush tukka and are very hard to harvest. The taste is quite salty, and you shouldn't eat too many because they can give you diarrhoea.

NATIVE MILKY OYSTER

ABORIGINAL NAME/S

Bandin – Djabugay tribe, Kuranda, Far North Queensland
Bidhiinja – Dharawal tribe

SCIENTIFIC NAME

Saccostrea cucullata

Native milky oysters grow in huddles or clusters on anything solid, from mangrove roots to reef shelves to rocky walls. They prefer to live in sheltered spots where the surface water is warm enough for them to spawn in summer. They can also be found in most estuaries and bays along the northern, eastern and southern coasts of Australia. Some grow up to 12cm in size and, if you're lucky, you can find oysters as big as a dinner plate!

There are many species of oyster, but be careful not to confuse native milky oysters with pearl oysters, which you can't eat because they are poisonous. You can tell them apart by the size and shape of the shells. Pearl oysters are typically larger, and round with a flat edge. Native milky oysters grow in little ear-shaped shells with lids, and they vary in size depending on whether they grow on rocks, mangroves, wooden or concrete pylons, or around boat ramps and jetties. The shells are generally grey with jagged, waved edges around the lid. Inside, the oyster body is cream but the gills are black and grey, and the shell is white and smooth.

You can neatly scrape them off rocks. Be careful not to crack an oyster directly on top, as that will squash the lid onto it. Instead, tap it from the side, and the lid will start to open. Once you have loosened the lid, remove the oyster – this can be tricky because its muscles are very strong! You can eat the oyster raw, straight from the shell, or cook it in its shell on hot coals.

TRADITIONAL USES

Native milky oysters are easy to harvest at low tide, and collecting them is fun. Oysters have always been a staple food for coastal saltwater Aboriginal People.

OTHER USES

Restaurants have many ways of serving native milky oysters. In the Western world, they are very expensive and highly prized.

Oysters are most nutritious when eaten raw, and have high levels of zinc, calcium and iron, as well as vitamins A and B12.

SALTWATER MUD MUSSEL

ABORIGINAL NAME/S

Djulwa – Djabugay tribe, Kuranda, Far North Queensland

SCIENTIFIC NAME

Polymesoda coaxans

These mussels prefer saltwater mud and mangrove environments. They like warm, dry climates and can be found at low tide, mostly around the north-western and north-eastern parts of Australia.

A mature mud mussel is 8–12cm long, and its shell features markings similar to the rings inside a tree's trunk. Mud mussels range in colour from black at the tip of the shell to brown and white around the base of the shell. Inside, the mussel is quite fleshy, but it shrinks to the size of a 20-cent piece when cooked.

To find saltwater mud mussels, look for large black shells sticking out of the mud, or small holes on the surface of the mud – the mussels breathe through these holes! Since they are usually buried deep in mangrove mudflats, you have to sit and dig in the mud with your hands to find them. If you're lucky, though, you'll find them on the mud's surface, as they make their way across it to find another home.

You can also find them in dry, cracked mud. Look out for a small, straight opening about 25mm long (as wide as a 20-cent coin), slightly covered in the mud. They're not easy to find, but once you know what you're looking for, you will start to see the landscape differently.

TRADITIONAL USES

Saltwater mud mussels are a delicacy for the northern Arnhem Land Yolŋu People. They are a valued food source for Indigenous saltwater people, providing high levels of protein, zinc, iron and vitamins.

Although different tribes call them different names, the hunting and cooking techniques are similar. After a day of gathering mussels in the mangroves, the Yolŋu People find a nice shady tree, light a fire and place them on the hot coals. After about 5 minutes, the shells start to open, and the mussels are ready to eat.

Another way the Yolŋu People like to cook mud mussels is to boil them in hot water. This gives the mussels a rubbery texture and a creamier taste. They also drink the warm, salty cooking water to get the rich minerals, which help the body fight colds and other viruses.

WITCHETTY GRUB

ABORIGINAL NAME/S

Maku – Anangu tribe, central Northern Territory

SCIENTIFIC NAME

Endoxyla leucomochla

It takes a brave soul to eat witchetty grubs without gagging! People think all Aboriginal People eat the grub and that it can be found everywhere, but bush tukka is specific to the Country you are from – so, if you were born in the desert, then you would most likely have been raised eating witchetty grubs.

Witchetty grubs are found in the roots of the river red gum, the witchetty bush, the small cooba and bloodwood trees in the central deserts of Australia.

These grubs are white with a yellow head and soft skin, and can grow to 1.5cm fat and 12cm long – that's even bigger than an adult human's thumb!

TRADITIONAL USES

Witchetty grubs are an important food for Aboriginal People in the desert. Only the women dig for them, and it's hard work. When they have collected enough, they light a fire and throw the grubs onto the hot coals, then cover them with hot ash to cook for about 5 minutes.

The grubs have a nutty flavour, and a texture very similar to warm scrambled eggs, but if eaten raw the grubs are soft and slimy with a sweet flavour. It's best to eat them whole, in one go!

OTHER USES

Witchetty grubs are so famous that everyone refers to them whenever bush tukka is mentioned, and some chefs use them to promote bush tukka in their restaurants. Everyone should try witchetty grubs at least once in their life!

I have chosen these special recipes just for you. Make sure you prepare and cook them with the guidance of an adult. Remember, adults should be responsible for anything involving sharp knives or hot ovens or pans.

RECIPES

BOUNCY KANGAROO BURGERS

This recipe tastes great! Kangaroo meat is so good for you – it will give you the fuel to bounce around like a kangaroo!

INGREDIENTS

- 500g kangaroo mince
- 1 red onion, peeled and chopped
- 2 tsp garlic salt
- 2 tbsp ground lemon myrtle
- 2 tbsp chicken salt (or plain salt)
- 1 egg
- olive oil
- 6 burger buns

- sauce ideas: mayonnaise, mustard, tomato sauce, BBQ sauce
- filling ideas: tomato, red onion, cheese, fried egg, lettuce

METHOD

1. To make the roo patties, put the kangaroo mince, chopped red onion, garlic salt, lemon myrtle and chicken salt in a bowl. Mix everything well.
2. Add your egg, and mix again until completely combined. (The egg acts as the binding agent to keep the patties together.)
3. Now shape your patties! Divide the mixture into six portions, then shape each portion into a patty and place on a plate, ready to cook.
4. With the help of an adult, heat the BBQ or frying pan to a high heat, add a dash of oil, and cook your patties until browned on both sides and cooked through.
5. To assemble your burgers, add your choice of sauce to a burger bun, then your patty and choice of fillings. Yum!

CROCODILE NUGGETS

We all enjoy the odd chicken nugget or two . . . but how about we try something new with snappy crocodile meat instead?

INGREDIENTS

- 2 eggs
- 1 cup cornflour
- 300g crocodile meat, diced
- 2 tbsp garlic powder
- 2 tbsp soy sauce
- 2 tbsp ground ginger
- 2 tbsp onion powder
- coconut oil (or oil of your choice)

METHOD

1. Beat the eggs in a small bowl and set aside. Put the cornflour in another small bowl and set aside.
2. Put the crocodile meat, garlic powder, onion powder, ground ginger and soy sauce into a food processor or blender. Blend until the meat is well minced, then place in a bowl.
3. Wet your hands with a little water, then take a small portion of the mince and roll it in your hands to make a ball. Place it on a clean tray and flatten into a nugget shape – or any shape you like! Repeat until you have used all the mince.
4. Using a pastry brush, coat the nuggets with the egg mixture then roll them gently in the cornflour. Place your nuggets on a tray and put in the fridge for 30 minutes.
5. Drizzle oil in the frying pan and heat, but be careful not to overheat the pan. Add your nuggets, leaving a bit of space around each one, and fry on both sides until golden and cooked through.
6. Remove nuggets from pan and place on a cooling rack.
7. Serve with BBQ or tomato sauce.

55 MIN

SERVES 4

SNAPPY CROC SKEWERS WITH PEANUT SAUCE

Crocodile meat is very moist! Just try not to overcook it, or it can get dry. You will need bamboo or metal skewers for this recipe – if you are using bamboo ones, soak them in water for a couple of hours first to stop them from burning.

INGREDIENTS

SKEWERS

- 300g crocodile meat, cut into strips
- 2 tbsp garlic powder
- 2 tbsp onion powder
- 3 tbsp crushed ginger
- 3 tbsp light soy sauce

SAUCE

- ¾ cup peanut butter (or tahini, if allergic to peanuts)
- ¼ cup white sugar
- 5–6 tbsp coconut milk
- ¼ cup apple cider vinegar or white vinegar
- 1 tbsp salt
- 3 tbsp light soy sauce

METHOD

Note: Soak bamboo skewer sticks in water before preparation.

1. Place all of the skewer ingredients in a bowl and mix. Place in the fridge for 30 minutes to marinate.
2. To make the peanut sauce, put all the sauce ingredients into a small saucepan and cook over medium-low heat for about 10 minutes. Make sure you keep stirring so that the mixture doesn't burn or stick to the bottom of the pan. Once cooked, set aside to cool, then put into a small serving bowl.
3. Remove the croc meat from the fridge and thread on to skewers – you should be able to fit 4–5 strips on each.
4. Heat the BBQ or a large nonstick pan over medium heat with a little oil. Cook the skewers in batches for 3–5 minutes on each side, until cooked through.
5. Serve with peanut sauce.

LEMON MYRTLE FISH AND CHIPS

This recipe involves dealing with extremely hot oil, so make sure an adult is in charge. The secret to not getting splattered with hot oil is to place the fish into the oil away from you – that way, any splatter will go away from you too!

INGREDIENTS

- 3 cups oil (peanut oil is good)
- 2 cups plain flour for batter mixture
- 4 tbsp ground lemon myrtle
- 1 tbsp garlic powder
- 1 tbsp onion powder
- 2 tbsp salt
- 1 tsp pepper (optional)

- 1 ½ cups soda water
- 1 cup flour for dry dipping
- 4–5 fish fillets (you can use barramundi, mackerel, snapper or perch)

METHOD

1. Heat the oil to 190°C in a deep-fryer, or a deep saucepan or frying pan. A cooking thermometer will help you make sure the oil stays at the right temperature and doesn't overheat, which will make your batter soggy and uncooked in the middle. You can also check your oil by dipping a wooden skewer in it. If the oil bubbles up around the skewer, it is the right temperature.
2. Put the flour, lemon myrtle, garlic powder, onion powder, salt and pepper in a large bowl and mix well.
3. Create a well in the middle, then add your soda water slowly. The batter will bubble up. Stir it well until nice and smooth, but not too runny. If the batter is too runny, it won't stick to the fish. Just add a bit more flour if you need to thicken it up.
4. Dip the pieces of fish into the 1 cup of dry flour, so they're completely covered in flour.
5. Dip a piece of fish into the batter until covered, then hold it over the bowl for a moment to let the excess batter drip off. Then add it gently to the hot oil by dipping and placing the fish away from you – try not to dump it. Cook for 3–4 minutes, or until the batter turns a nice golden-brown and the fish inside is cooked through. Place on a wire rack to rest and cool. Repeat this step with the remaining fish.
6. Serve with hot chips, salad and your favourite sauce!

BUSH TUKKA TRAIL MIX

This is a delicious snack that is perfect for a bush walk! For a sweeter blend you can add some honey, or for a more savoury blend try drizzling in some light soy sauce. Just make sure you check for anyone who has any allergies before sharing it with your friends.

INGREDIENTS

- 1 cup raw unsalted almonds
- 1 cup raw unsalted macadamia nuts
- 1 cup raw unsalted cashews
- 1 cup raw unsalted peanuts (optional)
- 1 cup sunflower seeds

- 1 cup pumpkin seeds
- 1 cup sultanas (optional)
- 2 tbsp ground lemon myrtle

METHOD

1. In a small bowl, mix all the nuts and seeds together well.
2. Heat a frying pan over medium heat, then add the nuts and seeds and roast until you see some colour. Toss regularly to avoid burning.
3. Return the nuts and seeds to the bowl. Add the sultanas and the lemon myrtle, and mix well until everything is coated. Set aside until cool, then store in paper bags or a glass jar, ready to eat.

LILLY PILLY POPSICLES

These delicious popsicles only need two ingredients and are so easy to make. They're a refreshing treat on a hot day. You can try making them with other ingredients too, like coconut milk and honey or even lemonade! You will need a popsicle tray for this recipe.

INGREDIENTS

- 1 cup lilly pillies
- 2 cups vanilla yoghurt

METHOD

1. Rinse your lilly pillies well, and remove the seeds. Then, with some help from an adult, chop and place them in a blender or food processor with the yoghurt. Blend until the mixture is how you like it – you can make a chunky blend or a smooth blend.

2. Pour the mixture into your popsicle tray, then place in the freezer overnight.

DID YOU KNOW?

There are more than 60 varieties of lilly pillies in Australia – and you can use any variety you like in this dish.

LEMON MYRTLE AND WATTLESEED GRANOLA BARS

Who doesn't love a yummy granola bar? Such a tasty and delicious snack! Adding lemon myrtle and wattleseed give these bars a twist of flavour that takes them to a different level. Make sure you check for allergies before sharing with friends.

INGREDIENTS

- ⅓ cup maple syrup or honey
- 1 tsp vanilla extract
- ½ cup honey
- ⅓ cup coconut oil, melted

- 3 cups rolled oats
- 1 cup chopped almonds
- ½ cup roasted peanuts, roughly chopped (optional)
- ½ cup dried apricots
- 1 cup puff buckwheat
- 1 cup macadamia nuts, roughly chopped
- 4 tbsp shaved coconut
- 4 tbsp ground lemon myrtle
- 4 tbsp ground wattleseeds

METHOD

1. Preheat the oven to 170°C fan-forced. Line a tray with baking paper.
2. In a small bowl, mix the maple syrup and honey, coconut oil and vanilla until combined.
3. In a larger bowl, mix all the remaining ingredients, then pour the honey mixture over and mix well until everything is combined.
4. Pour the mixture into the prepared tray and squish down with the back of a spoon to spread it out. Make sure the tray is covered evenly.
5. Bake in the oven for 30 minutes, or until golden-brown. Remove and allow to cool completely in the tray.
6. Once cool, put into the freezer and leave for an hour. Then remove from the freezer and place onto a chopping board, and use a sharp knife, with the help of an adult, to cut into bars, ready to serve.

WHERE TO BUY BUSH TUKKA

Kimberley Wild Gubinge
www.kimberleywildgubinge.com.au

Kakadu Plum Co
www.kakaduplum.com.au

My Dilly Bag
www.mydillybag.com.au

Australian Plants Online
www.australianplantsonline.com.au

Yuruga Nursery
yuruga.com.au

Tucker Bush
www.tuckerbush.com.au

MORE BUSH TUKKA RECIPES

Bush Food Shop
www.bushfoodshop.com.au

Bush Tucker Shop
www.bushtuckershop.com

Indigiearth
www.indigiearth.com.au

Tucker Bush
www.tuckerbush.com.au

Dreamtime Kullilla-Art
www.kullillaart.com.au

Taste Australia
www.tasteaustralia.biz

Oz Tukka
www.oztukka.com.au

Australian Native Food Co.
www.australiannativefoodco.com.au

MY THANKS TO YOU

I want to extend my sincere gratitude to the amazing team at Hardie Grant for providing me with an incredible opportunity to write the *Bush Tukka Guide for Kids*.

Working on this book has been a truly rewarding journey, allowing me to discover and share the extraordinary world of bush foods with young readers. I am deeply grateful for the support and enthusiasm from everyone involved, which has made this guide possible. I hope that this book inspires curiosity, respect for nature, and a sense of adventure in children across Australia.

Throughout the writing process, I was constantly inspired by the resilience and wisdom found in our country and communities. Every step – from researching ancient practices to gathering stories from Elders – revealed just how much bush foods are woven into the fabric of daily life and cultural identity. I am honoured to have listened to and learned from those who generously shared their knowledge, and I have done my best to ensure their voices are respectfully represented throughout these pages.

At times this journey was humbling, reminding me of the responsibility that comes with sharing stories that are not only nourishing to the mind but also to the spirit. I hope young readers will approach these pages with wonder and openness – ready to learn not only what grows in the wild, but how every leaf, seed and root is part of a living story that continues to shape who we are today.

I have been reminded of the profound connections between people, land and culture that bush foods embody. Each plant and ingredient tells a story, shaped by generations of knowledge and stewardship from First Nations communities. Looking ahead, I am excited to see how the *Bush Tukka Guide for Kids* will find its way into homes, classrooms and communities – sparking conversations about the native foods that flourish all around us. I envision this book not only as a resource, but as an invitation: for families to forage together, for teachers to incorporate bush tukka into learning, and for children to experience the joy of tasting something new that has grown in their own backyard.

May this guide serve as a bridge, connecting the old ways with the present, and empowering the next generation to be custodians of our natural world. To everyone who turns these pages, thank you for joining me on this journey of discovery. Together, we can nurture a deeper appreciation for the land, its stories, and the generations who have cared for it long before us – and who will continue to do so, guided by curiosity and respect, far into the future.

Including traditional names in this book is a crucial part of working towards preserving and sharing Aboriginal culture. We can all stand proud for playing our part in keeping culture strong. I thank you!

Published in 2026 by Hardie Grant Explore, an imprint of Hardie Grant Publishing

Hardie Grant Explore (Melbourne)
Wurundjeri Country
Level 11, 36 Wellington Street
Collingwood, Victoria 3066

Hardie Grant Explore (Sydney)
Gadigal Country
Level 7, 45 Jones Street
Ultimo, NSW 2007

hardiegrant.com/explore

A catalogue record for this book is available from the National Library of Australia

Hardie Grant acknowledges the Traditional Owners of the Country on which we work, the Wurundjeri People of the Kulin Nation and the Gadigal People of the Eora Nation, and recognises their continuing connection to the land, waters and culture. We pay our respects to their Elders past and present.

For all relevant publications, Hardie Grant Explore commissions a First Nations consultant to review relevant content and provide feedback to ensure suitable language and information is included in the final book. Hardie Grant Explore also includes traditional place names and acknowledges Traditional Owners, where possible, in both the text and mapping for their publications.

Traditional place names are included in palawa kani, the language of Tasmanian Aboriginal People, with thanks to the Tasmanian Aboriginal Centre.

Bush Tukka Guide for Kids
ISBN 9781741179163

10 9 8 7 6 5 4 3 2 1

Publishers
Tahlia Anderson, Amanda Louey

Project Editor
Lauren Carta

Editors
Kimberley Davis, Irma Gold

First Nations Consultant
Tribal Voice Connections

Education Consultant
Kristina Schulz

Design
Cause/Affect

Cartography
Emily Maffei

Typesetting
Kerry Cooke

Production Manager
Simone Wall

Illustration on p. xxvii by Cause/Affect

Colour reproduction by Splitting Image Colour Studio

Printed in China by LEO Paper Products LTD.

The paper this book is printed on is from FSC®-certified forests and other controlled sources. FSC® promotes environmentally responsible, socially beneficial and economically viable management of the world's forests.

Publisher's Disclaimer

The information shared in this book is for educational purposes, and readers engage in activities at their own risk.

Certain native and introduced plants can be highly toxic and in some cases consuming them can be fatal. The author and publisher take no responsibility for any illness, injury or damages brought on through consuming or handling plants or animals.

Readers are advised that it is their responsibility to ensure they are not trespassing on Aboriginal land, or contravening laws or regulations by disturbing fauna or flora in national parks or on crown or private land.